NEW GLOBAL ALLIANCES: INSTITUTIONS, ALIGNMENTS AND LEGITIMACY IN THE CONTEMPORARY WORLD

A Convoco Edition

CORINNE MICHAELA FLICK (ED.)

Convoco! Editions

Convoco Foundation
Brienner Strasse 28
D – 80333 Munich
www.convoco.co.uk

British Library Cataloguing-in-Publication data: a catalogue
record for this book is available from the British Library.

Edited by Dr. Corinne Michaela Flick
Translated from German by Philippa Hurd
Layout and typesetting by Jill Sawyer Phypers

Printed and bound in Great Britain by Clays Ltd, Elcograf S.p.A.

ISBN: 978-1-9163673-2-6

Previously published Convoco titles:

The Standing of Europe in the New Imperial World Order (2020)

The Multiple Futures of Capitalism (2019)

The Common Good in the 21st Century (2018)

Authority in Transformation (2017)

Power and its Paradoxes (2016)

To Do or Not To Do—Inaction as a Form of Action (2015)

Dealing with Downturns: Strategies in Uncertain Times (2014)

Collective Law-Breaking—A Threat to Liberty (2013)

Who Owns the World's Knowledge? (2012)

**Can't Pay, Won't Pay? Sovereign Debt and the Challenge of
Growth in Europe (2011)**

For perhaps the first time in history, people around the world are having the same conversations and sharing the same fears... It might only be for this weird moment in our history, but we cannot deny that we are currently experiencing what it feels like to live in One World.

Ivan Krastev (2020)

CONTENTS

INTRODUCTION

Dear Friends of Convoco,

Back in 2019, when Convoco's topic for 2020, *New Global Alliances: Institutions, Alignments, and Legitimacy in the Contemporary World* was formed, the changes that would affect us all over the last twelve months were barely perceptible. Now, it is obvious how much this topic reflects the current state of our world and registers our new awareness. As a result of COVID-19, the new collaborations and connections have become much more visible, and a new sense of solidarity is being expressed transnationally. The value of the common good has become clearer and has taken on a global character. More than ever, the nation state is no longer an exclusive point of reference. But that does not mean that we are not also seeing the emergence of strong national interests. These contrasting developments go hand in hand. At first glance they seem to be mutually exclusive, but the coexistence of paradoxes is a crucial feature of the new era.[1]

We are seeing more and more transnational initiatives. Topics such as climate change, environmental pollution, and pandemics do not recognize national borders and therefore require greater cooperation from the global community. Transnational movements in civil society, which have been such a prominent feature of the year 2020, are an expression of a new sense of responsibility for the dangers threatening our planet, and an awareness of our collective interdependence. At state level, we can see new forms of international cooperation. While multilateralism (the system whereby multiple states all agree to a common agenda) is coming under pressure in many places, new formations of "plurilateralism" (in which states make agreements limited to particular regions and issues) are emerging. In East Asia, including Indonesia and Australia, the world's largest free trade area, the Regional Comprehensive Economic Partnership (RCEP), has been set up under China's leadership. This Asia–Pacific alliance puts less emphasis on climate and labor issues or the free movement of people, emphasizing instead the simplification of regional supply chains by reducing tariffs.

We are seeing partnerships between stakeholders who have not worked together before. For example, governments and private actors are cooperating in areas that were originally sovereign. This is particularly evident in information technology. Equally, in the so-called "Track II diplomacy," NGOs and other non-state actors function as mediators in conflicts where the international community is increasingly unable to find solutions.

These partnerships and alliances have also been joined by a new group of non-state actors: private philanthropists deploying resources on an unprecedented scale. The "tech activist" is an entirely new phenomenon. Entrepreneurs such as Bill Gates and Michael Bloomberg are taking global responsibility for aspects of issues such as health and the environment. Such transnational influence, however well-intentioned, can be a double-edged sword. In the Bill & Melinda Gates Foundation, for example, the ambivalent role of many of these new non-state actors becomes clear: on the one hand, they are bridge-builders whose networking activities are applauded, and on the other hand they are largely unaccountable foreign actors who are influencing the political agenda. This raises fundamental questions about the legitimacy of these new actors and the alliances that are suddenly emerging alongside our traditional global institutions. They claim a legitimacy that is derived from their self-defined task, "whether it be [...] from moral authority, expertise, or the critical oversight of pressing issues such as energy supply or environmental protection in civil society."[2] How this differs from paternalism or even neocolonialism is not always immediately clear.

The UN Secretary-General António Guterres has offered some words of caution:

> The nations that came out on top more than seven decades ago [i.e. in 1945] have refused to contemplate the reforms needed to change power relations in international institutions. [...] A new model for global governance must be based on full, inclusive, and equal participation in global institutions.[3]

It will take statesmanship and leadership from the world powers to revive our existing institutions. Bearing in mind the increasingly isolationist attitude of the United States, however, there is little hope that we can expect this from the West's traditional leading power in the near future. This is unlikely to change even under the new presidency; we have seen a turning away from Europe since President Obama's term of office. However, this situation offers Europe an opportunity to fill the vacuum and assume more global responsibility, provided that Europe is able to develop in a more united fashion. There are many ways in which Europe can achieve more cooperation; it is now a matter of implementing these ideas.

Institutions are an important factor in creating a stable world order: they are instruments of cooperation. At their best, institutions combine a long-term purpose with an understanding of the common good and create a sense of collective responsibility.[4] They collate the experiences of many people across generations and can transform opposites into a unified whole. Institutions are therefore an important tool for "civilizing" the world; or, in other words, for creating a world in which different cultures coexist equally, a world that is committed to common rules and relies on universal cooperation—and which recognizes that a hegemonic power is not necessary. The essays in this volume argue that this is the way in which our understanding of the world should develop. The crisis triggered by the pandemic can help us to do this, because—in the words of the famous Chinese proverb—every crisis also offers an opportunity. The pandemic makes it clear how our own wellbeing depends on the wellbeing of others.

In 1986 the sociologist Ulrich Beck described the place of "solidarity" on the path towards a new modern era. He spoke of a "risk society" that operates together on the basis of shared risks. For Beck, this leads to the creation of solidarity based on fear. The macro-sociologist Heinz Bude describes solidarity as emerging from the feeling of vulnerability that arises from an experience such as the threat posed by the COVID-19 virus.[5] The universality and supranationality of today's challenges can lead to a global community of solidarity based on a shared perception of a common threat.

But there is also a more altruistic form of trans-national solidarity that has been witnessed in recent years that derives from a sense of a shared humanity that transcends nation, race, and creed and inspires compassion for the sufferings of our fellow men and women. This has been seen in the international charitable response to major natural disasters; in the successful prosecutions of perpetrators of human rights abuses and "crimes against humanity"; and in the extensive international outrage at the extra-judicial killing of Blacks by the police in the United States. This universalist sense of solidarity is being encountered more and more frequently. We are experiencing it, for example, in the numerous move-ments demanding greater equality and justice between different social groups across national borders. This is a new kind of "inclusive solidarity," in contrast to what used to be its most frequently encountered form: an externally differentiating type of solidarity in the spirit of "us against the rest of the world." As Heinz Bude has termed it recently, this new form of inclusive solidarity embodies "the riddle of a special kind of complicity that can claim no solid basis, but rather is an existential experience in itself."[6]

This emergent "global community of solidarity" includes not only human beings and their welfare but has also extended to include concerns about the animal and plant worlds. Here, too, a process of transformation is underway, which is becoming more and more apparent in the global shift towards renewable energies and in the adoption of such practices as CO_2-certificate trading. The alternative, we are now frequently reminded, is a new age of mass extinctions, possibly including humankind itself.

It is already becoming apparent that the road towards an ideal of universal cooperation might also be one strewn with conflicts to come. It is already clear that the unilateral world order of the last decades no longer applies. But it is far from clear as to what will replace it. Is our world now bipolar or rather multipolar? Or are we on the road to a "post-hegemonic" age in which the geopolitical world no longer revolves around historic "poles"? Our difficulty in finding an answer to these questions is already proof enough that something new is emerging. Meanwhile, the virus is acting as a catalyst for transformation. COVID-19 carries the risk of exacerbating existing inequalities in the world. Regions that were already hungry and poor before the pandemic might fall further behind in their development and their societies become more vulnerable. This would widen the already existing gulf between countries and increase the risk of the world falling apart. That cannot be in anyone's interest. Today's challenges demand new and enhanced forms of cooperation and collaboration as they arise. They are based on a growing understanding of the common good.

Corinne Michaela Flick, January 2021

Notes

1. Convoco Notes, "How should we understand the new nationalism?" *Newsletter*, October 4, 2020. https://mailchi. mp/248652b98997/cuso7qcxlg-4450186?e=6606e80255 (accessed January 8, 2021)

2. Stefan Korioth, "Legitimacy in the New World Order" in this present volume, p. 41.

3. António Guterres, "Tackling the inequality pandemic: a new social contract for a new era," Nelson Mandela Annual

Lecture, New York 2020, https://www.nelsonmandela. org/news/entry/annual-lecture-2020-secretary-general-guterress-full-speech (accessed January 8, 2021).

4. Roger Scruton, "Being and Letting Be" in Corinne Michaela Flick (ed.), *To Do or Not To Do: Inaction as a Form of Action* (Munich: Convoco Editions, 2015), pp. 29–43.

5. Heinz Bude and Corinne Flick, "Solidarität aus Verwundbarkeit," CONVOCO! Podcast (23), September 2020, http://convoco.co.uk/de/convoco-podcast-heinz-bude-1 (accessed January 8, 2021).

6. Heinz Bude, *Solidarität: Die Zukunft einer großen Idee* (Munich: Carl Hanser, 2019), p. 33.

THESES

CORINNE MICHAELA FLICK

As a result of COVID-19, the new collaborations and connections have become much more visible, and a new sense of solidarity is being expressed transnationally. The value of the common good has become clearer and has taken on a global character. More than ever, the nation state is no longer an exclusive point of reference. But that does not mean that we are not also seeing the emergence of strong national interests. These contrasting developments go hand in hand. At first glance they seem to be mutually exclusive, but the coexistence of paradoxes is a crucial feature of the new era.

STEFAN OSCHMANN

I consider it essential that we consciously combine our diverse strengths, perspectives, and methods to ensure healthy future prospects for everyone. As a global community, we need stronger, multilateral solidarity, and considerably more partnerships that extend across sectors. After all, we are facing serious global risks and there is little that a single country or group can do to combat them on its own.

UDO DI FABIO

A new alliance of political officials and actors in civil society must overcome the new, paralyzing political thinking in camps, not with the aim of creating a new conformity, but rather the other way round—with the aim of launching a new culture of debate.

CLEMENS FUEST

From the societal point of view, productive alliances between politics and business should not primarily mean interdependencies and close cooperation between representatives of business and political decision-makers, but rather a shared awareness of the rules that must be adhered to so that the individual profit-seeking really serves the common good.

WOLFGANG SCHÖN

A "world government" that no one can escape from is an horrific thought while acknowledging the fantastic, technocratic opportunities it presents for overcoming global challenges. But the creation of a "global community" whose members feel bound together by a sense of solidarity and who bind national and international institutions to the aims of a global common good would constitute a great step forward.

EUGÉNIA C. HELDT

International institutions find themselves under increasing public pressure. Against this backdrop I argue that international organizations are the tragic heroes of international politics, because if they work too closely with the member states, they are seen as puppets controlled by the most powerful states in the system. If, on the other hand, they emancipate themselves and act on their own initiative, they are accused of abuse of power.

STEFAN KORIOTH

For a long time, a system's legitimacy related exclusively to clearly defined societies, generally organized in the form of states. These closed circles of legitimacy have been circumvented by competitors. A growing number of supranational and global private organizations claim legitimacy alongside or against the state for sectoral activities and also when making decisions about how the economy is organized. However, it remains the task of states to recognize or reject claims to legitimacy.

MAHA HOSAIN AZIZ

The 2010s saw the world experience a unique global legitimacy crisis, as perceived norms in geopolitics, politics, economy, and society were challenged. This legitimacy crisis will likely deepen in the 2020s all over the world.

RUDOLF MELLINGHOFF

Civil society organizations play an important role in the political process. Through their participation they can make a legitimate contribution to political decisions, in particular at international level. However, the final binding decision on sovereign measures must still be left to democratically legitimized institutions.

CHRISTOPH G. PAULUS

The first, young alliance of European states is already in danger of collapse once more. In order to stop this, we must create a new narrative since Europe has lost its persuasive power and attraction as a bringer and guarantor of peace. We might reap this new narrative from the COVID-19 crisis, namely a Europe of common rights and responsibilities.

SVEN SIMON

China has turned into a systemic rival, competing with the West in its promise of prosperity. In light of China's increasing political and economic importance, the Western liberal democracies throughout the world should form a strategic alliance, the D10 (ten democracies), in order to be able to survive this systemic competition.

GISBERT RÜHL

Digitalization is having a huge impact on the world of work and on the business models of major companies—digital platforms are the business model of the 21st century. Europe can only counter the supremacy of Chinese and American companies by creating an innovation-friendly infrastructure and by adopting a common approach to make sure it can compete.

BAZON BROCK

Re-thinking the oldest notion—capitalism is on the wane.

GARRETT WALLACE BROWN

Beyond health-systems thinking we have to also start thinking about factors like planetary health, ecological systems, and environmental determinants of human health. We need joined-up thinking that looks at global health as a system, with corresponding functions and delivery mechanisms.

LOTHAR H. WIELER

The more solidarity the global community can show in the distribution of vaccines, the sooner adequate immunity can be achieved across individual countries. With both immunity and preparedness, the same principle applies: the weakest link in the chain determines the success of all.

TIMO MEYNHARDT

It is unclear whether the pandemic will lead to new constellations of the common good. But one thing is certain: the heyday of differentiation theorists is over if the latter do not take account of their assumptions about the common good. A reversal of the point of departure is required.

JÖRN LEONHARD

Identifying a turning point involves pinning down the pluperfect tense. However, the COVID-19 pandemic does not yet have a definable *ancien régime*. Nevertheless, the multitude of paradoxes increases the likelihood of a world in upheaval, between transition and transformation, not created through a revolution in a single moment, but incrementally through the gradual unfolding and ever longer duration of the crisis. Today we can no longer be as certain as we were a year ago that something completely new isn't emerging from beneath the surface of the supposedly familiar, the apparently repetitive, the prefigured present, breaking through the hermeneutical framework of the narrative of continuity.

CHAPTER 1

THE NEW GEOPOLITICAL CONSTELLATION: CONFLICTS OF LEGITIMACY BETWEEN INSTITUTION AND ACTION

UDO DI FABIO

No one can deny it—we are living among new geopolitical alliances. The multilateral Atlantic world order, which has prevailed for 70 years, is in decline.

Under the generally benevolent hegemony of the United States, a distinctive process of internationalization had been developing since 1945. International organizations from the UN, the EU, ASEAN, the IMF, NATO, the WTO, and the OECD to international courts of justice are foregrounding the world of supranational politics. On this basis, the old power-states [*Machtstaaten*] have allowed themselves to become increasingly interdependent. The ongoing primary areas of national politics were moderated and structured by an increasingly dense network of treaties and international organizations. The states' aspirations to absolute sovereignty (in theory at least) were relativized by the principle of mutual commitments. At international conferences or European Council meetings, common goals were formulated, agreements made, and compromises reached. The focus was on ensuring open trade routes and fair trading conditions, currency and economic issues, arms limitation, collective peace-keeping, and containment of the consequences of war. It was about cross-border issues such as education, combating epidemics, securing the world's food supply, protecting species, the global climate, and the debate about social or ecological projects. Today, all of this has converged to form a supranational agenda. Over the course of decades, institutions of "global government" have been consolidated.[1]

After the end of the Cold War it looked as though "global government" was not just a no-nonsense technical description of an intergovernmental culture of conferences and negotiations, but had what it took to create a form of world government and gradually bring about the end of states as the determining subjects of history. In his philosophical sketch, *Perpetual Peace*, the astute late-Enlightenment thinker Immanuel Kant had conceptually explored the two paths towards civilized state relations or a unified world republic.[2] Earlier, Thomas Hobbes had justified the modern absolutist state of the 17th century, legitimizing it through an image of human existence in the state of nature in which each individual is at war against the other, and the law of the stronger (that is, no law) prevails. Accordingly, freedom for Hobbes, understood as applying to individuals, was only possible if one entered the state of legality under the rule of law and the rule of a holder of the monopoly of power—the Leviathan. Kant then applied this rational, reasonable legitimization of the state to a higher level—the world of states. In this world of sovereign states, the unbridled law of the stronger originally dominates too—through the doctrine of *jus ad bellum*, the right to war. The process of civilizing states through to the international prohibition of violence[3] is a process that also establishes legality between states and gradually creates guarantees of such legality.[4] But Immanuel Kant has not simply taken Hobbes' ideas one level higher from the world of individuals to the world of states. The Königsberg philosopher's ideas go a little deeper than those of political realist Thomas Hobbes. For if Kant had remained true to the Hobbesian model as he moved up a level, he would have had to posit a global state, a world Leviathan in terms of the philosophy of reason. But that is exactly what Kant did not do. Although he sees the substance of everyone's global civil rights in the international peace imperative, he even considers war between states to be the lesser evil by comparison with a world state, which in its functionally necessary abstraction from all real living conditions and in view of the right of political communities to self-determination could only result in "soulless despotism."[5]

Nevertheless, since 1990 we might get the impression that an international elite network was vigorously promoting a project of disestablishment and denationalization in favor of new forms of government. Today, some misguided souls consider foreign politicians and diplomats, intellectuals and entrepreneurs, NGOs and scientific advisors, officials of the EU Commission and OECD experts, or global political foundations and judges at international courts to be part of a network of secret societies with an agenda that is potentially destructive, or at least not democratically legitimate. During the Enlightenment, traditional supporters of the absolute monarchy or the corporative state must have regarded the Freemasons with equal suspicion. Today names such as "Bilderberg Conference," George Soros, or Bill and Melinda Gates are bandied about by every self-respecting conspiracy theorist.

But there is no dark conspiracy. What has existed for decades was and is a rationally justified agreement and well-intentioned cosmopolitan common sense, according to which every step towards supranationally strengthened commitments is justified precisely because of the risk of the atavistic power-state flaring up once again. Any mechanism for integrating states was considered good, and any reinforcement of mutual dependencies was considered positive. At the end of a marathon negotiation in Brussels in late July 2020, France's President Macron was not only able to justify assuming a joint burden of debt to deal with COVID-19 aid measures as a necessary evil, but he was also able to celebrate it as an historic step.

The constraints involved in previous steps towards integration, conceived as future-proof elements of denationalization, such as the monetary union or the common asylum policy, are now proving to have an impact that creates pressure to remove the boundaries of traditional institutions, such as democracy, parliamentary budgetary powers, the stability of currencies, or that of the financial markets. Internal and external factors are strangely intertwined. The global economy offers enormous advantages, but as an exogenous, unmanageable process it can also cause considerable difficulties in adaptation and bring about costs within states. Governments react to global (exogenous) uncertainties by increasing their public spending on social welfare in the domestic economy. If greater economic integration then leads to greater global insecurity, this can destroy the benefits of globalization.[6] The same is true from a cultural perspective.[7] The architects of supranationalism have good reason to see themselves as representatives of the Enlightenment and as pioneers of universal human rights and global common interests. But today they are up against reactive powers of opposition.

But who exactly were the actors in this multilateral world order that is now falling apart? The important actors on this stage were the states' diplomatic staff, but also international scientific organizations, global companies, private aid funds, economic interest groups, and politically oriented non-governmental organizations. The great process of globalization took place within this framework, the latter itself gradually becoming more stable and established practice. Under Cold War conditions, this multilateral framework was always precarious. But its ritualistic processes and

standards of behavior nevertheless stood for a predom-
inant trend that was linear and powerful. As has been
shown both sociologically and socio-psychologically,
over decades an international elite has emerged that
sees itself as progressive within its states and its national
cultural arenas and works towards disciplining the
egotism of the state.[8] This project is about civilizing the
old power-states through new forms of rational political cooperation and law-making.

But history seldom operates in a linear way. It does
not always travel along a rational path of progress. The
trend towards internationalization existed and still
coexists with that of resilience—the tenacity and inertia
of national and regional domains of rulership. The
treachery within the dialectical course of history can
lie in the fact that even the best forces can conjure up
opposing forces which—if they are powerful enough—
can certainly distract from the "path of progress." This
can also be traced back to genuine conditions of political rulership, which are dependent on strong patterns
of identity, especially in situations of tension or centrif-
ugal forces—feelings of community whose provenance
is cultural, linguistic, socio-structural, family, ethnic,
or (time and again) religious.[9]

In addition, there is a dangerous loss of knowledge about institutions. Anyone who understands the

state only in its aberrant form as the power-state of the great world wars and sees it as a danger to peace and the goals of the global common good may miss the enormous potential of this modern form of rulership. The institution of the modern state had reduced the complexity of the political system. Concentration of state power, a professional civil service, rational ruler-ship through codified law, and belief in scientific, tech-nical, and social progress—these are all characteristics of the modern state. In the democratic constitutional state in particular, an institution emerged that could be seen—even in a functionally differentiated society—as the focus of society that was capable of taking action. This is a focus legitimized by the *volonté générale* of its citizens and by their continued consent through elec-tions and polls (Art. 20 (2) sentence 2 Basic Law).[10]

But the increasing efficiency of the state, its plural-istic, domestic openness, and the opening up of the German state to the outside that took place after 1945 and then after 1990 increased the complexity of the political system once more. The internal pluralization of liberal societies and their external confederation, especially in supranational Europe, banished the threat of dictatorship and war in a highly effective way. But governing transnationally while maintaining national and regional legislation and administration made politics enormously complicated.

The reality of political rulership today is once again reminiscent of pre-modern models that the rational state had at one time transcended. EU reforms or changes to the US electoral system, for example, are about as "simple" as fundamental social and economic reform in ancient imperial China or the reorganization of the financial and military system in the medieval Holy Roman Empire. The highly differentiated horizontal and vertical separation of powers is not the only cause. Political logjams and an erosion of institutions can also be observed in countries without a supranational tradition, such as the United States. On the one hand, the space of public opinion is globalized and universally focused with its emphasis on human rights, diversity, and a global agenda for the common good. In the liberal, progressive section of the political spectrum, the sense of community is abstracted into global relationships and at the same time parceled out into group identities of diverse thinking. The political left is far-reaching in its cosmopolitan and universal attitudes, and at the same time equally particularizing and divisive in terms of ecological locality and its group-specific emphasis on identity. The conservative, right wing of the political system continues to look for communities in cultural or national realms of experience and adopts a global perspective as a geopolitical theme of national self-assertion and building a world order. Both major political directions divide the space of public opinion "provincially" and even tribally—albeit in different ways—internally it is increasingly fractured into fragmented spaces of experience.

Equally, the political ambition to control creates enormous complexity. It reduces the possibilities of observing relevant real life, simply because too much is happening that is objectively complicated. The relentless attempt to control society using laws and regulations or even to transform it completely, the attempt to combat economic crises and imbalances through fiscal and monetary interventions, has led to oppressive overregulation and a hybridization of the financial and fiscal economy that stretched old institutions such as the banking system and central bank policy to their limits. Such pressure to remove boundaries exists not only in the EU, but also in Japan, Brazil, and North America. In their *Dialogues on Development*, the Indian political philosophers Ramashray Roy and Raj Kamal Srivastava have identified the machinery of political legislation's inability to rein itself in and impose self-discipline as its greatest disadvantage: "The greatest drawback of our rulers is their lack of

THE NEW GEOPOLITICAL CONSTELLATION

discipline. They cannot maintain discipline among themselves nor can they maintain discipline over their administrative machinery."[11]

In a theoretically challenging sense, politics is not simply legislation and the enforcement of laws through administration. Political rulership takes place in an open and networked process of communication in which the goals of the common good are debated and which focuses on the enforcement of obedience only at the end of a long process. For example, a climate protection conference debates whether the target of two degrees by the end of the century is a sensible project capable of achieving consensus; international organizations and supranational institutions such as the EU then align themselves with this and individual states commit themselves accordingly through national regulations or by accepting emissions trading schemes through international treaties. Transnational reason pursues such large projects, thereby becoming legitimized by their substance and the telos of history.

Those who combat global hunger, the oppression of women in underdeveloped societies, who fight illiteracy, child mortality and epidemics, global warming and its consequences are objectively and morally legitimized. The legitimacy of international projects, the intrinsic value of cooperation, and the expert authority of institutions such as the World Health Organization (WHO) appeared more and more alongside the classic legitimacy of international legal commitments. Groups of experts and political actors from NGOs or private foundations such as Melinda and Bill Gates linked up with international organizations. In addition to the usual diplomatic intergovernmental conferences, a supranational arena for communication and action came into being, which influenced the policy-making of state and international bodies, even providing assistance with complementary or proactive campaigns, for example in dealing with famine, promoting development, schooling, or the consequences of climate change. After the end of the Cold War, this one-world alliance operated as the indisputable matrix of a universal world order. The spirit of the world republic pervaded intellectual and media discourse.

The technical reality and dissemination of the World Wide Web seemed to be a coincidence in technological, political, and structural terms. In the early 1990s the US Vice-President Al Gore talked about the "digital agora." The dream of a global democracy and completely new forms of participation seemed possible; by contrast, thinking in terms of constitutional and international legal categories seemed old-fashioned. Even major, established democracies such as England were only to be conceived as regulatory frameworks geared to global interests of the common good and institutionally engaged. The global network looked like the keystone of the logos of history. At the start of the second decade of this century, many saw the Arab Spring as a necessary and logical uprising of young people who organized their rebellion using social networks.[12] As early as 2014, mass demonstrations of overwhelmingly young people using their smartphones had become the symbol of the digital agora, which seemed to turn every national and territorial claim to rulership into a hopeless undertaking.[13]

The development of a normatively and institutionally integrated form of sovereignty has been approaching its limits for a long time, however. What we are experiencing today is a rebellion against this system—a serious "counterrevolution." In this struggle, new geopolitical alliances are emerging. China accepted the Atlantic system as a condition of its own economic advancement only as a default position, but never wanted to become part of this system. Ancient China was Sinocentric, regarding its neighbors as mere vassals. When the Europeans destroyed China in the 19th century through their principles of trade and the formal equality of states, the Chinese called them "unequal treaties," and they remain an important

31

memory that informs Beijing's policy to this day. The tanks on Tiananmen Square in 1989 sent a clear signal that China will neither liberalize nor democratize domestically, and that it will not allow itself to be unilaterally integrated with the outside world either. China's priorities are harmony, reputation, and the self-assertion of its community—not the centrality of universal human rights. In China, the Party and the state have classified the universal claims of the liberal worldview as a subversive threat.[14] The more powerful China becomes, the more the United States jeopardizes its hegemonic position, and the longer Europe remains incapable of establishing itself as an independent global power, the more significantly the balance of geopolitical power mechanisms will shift.[15]

Since Putin came to power and since Erdoğan adopted his neo-Ottoman, autocratic policies in Turkey, the number of anti-Western players has increased. The multilateral world has become a multipolar world. Equally, the Western democracies are losing the stability that made them strong during the Cold War. The United States is internally divided, provocations appear from right and left, rifts are being deepened. Even beyond Trump, "America First" is likely to remain on the agenda of the old global power. Brexit took place under the emotive slogan of "Take back control."[16] For the public sphere of opinion in continental Europe, this was typical English quirkiness, perhaps even the result of an internally and externally controlled manipulation of the referendum; in any case it was seen as a completely incomprehensible deviation from the secure road of reason. But that half of the British public who voted for Brexit wanted above all their own democratic self-determination back and rejected an ever closer union. This was also a rejection of a project that had once been launched with significant participation from the United Kingdom and which now stands at a fork in the road.[17] Should we carry on and keep our head down? Or do new alliances have to be forged in order to escape the trap of a new friend/enemy distinction?

Anyone who is really serious about global projects today has to recognize the conditions underpinning any kind of political action. Moral and factual discourses are always tied to institutional contexts. Those who uncompromisingly adopt a morally or factually well-grounded position can deserve respect. But if they espouse their position in such a way that the institutions of constitutional democracies are damaged, then they are violating the basic conditions of political morality. For example, there are very good reasons to call for the phasing-out of coal-fired power.

But there is no single good reason to use force against police officers in a democracy.[18] Young people's anger over what they believe to be a lack of climate change policy is legitimate. But the assertion that an entire generation has failed or that parliament has been subverted by lobbyists is a repudiation of democracy. In the migration crisis that began in 2015, states or the vast majority of citizens who were critical of borders being opened without controls were not rogue states or inhuman people, and not unchristian. But the moral mechanism of forming friend/enemy camps snapped shut like a trap. Opposing political opinions must be explored and sustained more vigorously before the guillotine of moral condemnation falls. Those who violate people's dignity or stir up violence and hatred deserve the disregard and possibly the harshness of the rule of law. But debates must be conducted openly beyond these limits—without prematurely turning one's opponent into an enemy or an evil-doer using the mechanisms of a politically skewed morality. A new alliance of political officials and actors in civil society must overcome this new, paralyzing political thinking in camps, not with the aim of creating a new conformity, but rather the other way round—with the aim of launching a new culture of debate.

The new geopolitical alliances force us to rethink. The democracies will have to invest more in themselves, in the vitality and functionality of their states, so that they can invest in the application of human rights and in the public goods of humanity worldwide. A policy that is prepared to rethink will take the ability to act and the self-assertion of institutions much more seriously again and connect it to every kind of subject. The wisdom of the centuries is preserved in institutions. We know that free world trade was a prerequisite for world peace not only for Immanuel Kant. We know that the market economy, especially the social market economy, is far superior to any state-determined command economy. We know that without an effective rule of law individual freedom is impossible. Nobody should lag behind John Locke, the state philosopher of the Enlightenment and American independence, and believe that one could trade peace for freedom or vice versa. And nobody should believe that in the long run peace and equitable prosperity can flourish based on lack of freedom.

The rule of law is one of the fundamental institutions.[19] The independence of the courts is just as important as respect for public servants who have been appointed by democracy. Police officers, firefighters, and paramedics are bound by the law and therefore require legal and public oversight; but they are also entitled to expect effective protection if they are attacked. Political culture that loses respect in this regard loses one of its lifelines. Political judgment requires the ability to contextualize and to create sociocultural sustainability. Those who want a sustainable democracy will not only invest in climate protection but also balance the national budget and not let democratic responsibility for the budget dissolve into uncertain joint debt securities like sugar cubes in hot tea. Sustainable politics promotes pioneering technological achievements and a competitive edge. It recognizes education and social integration in the labor market as a prerequisite for a society based on solidarity.

Individual freedom, our innate human rights, to which everyone is equally entitled, form one bond in a normative double helix that coexists with another strand of information.[20] This other bond is collective, political freedom, i.e. popular sovereignty, communal self-determination—both converge while remaining distinct in one ordered constitutional state. These two genetic codes of individual self-development and communal self-determination are never identical but they belong together and they are the prerequisite for the West's ability to assert itself in a new geopolitical constellation, which at the end of the day will result in a new balanced and peaceful order.

Notes

1. Joel P. Trachtman, *The Future of International Law: Global Government* (Cambridge: Cambridge University Press, 2013).

2. Immanuel Kant, *Perpetual Peace: A Philosophical Sketch*, http://fs2.american.edu/dfagel/www/Class%20Readings/Kant/Immanuel%20Kant,%20_Perpetual%20Peace_.pdf (accessed December 14, 2020).

3. "All Members shall refrain in their international relations from the threat or use of force against the territorial integrity or political independence of any state, or in any other manner inconsistent with the Purposes of the United Nations." *Charter of the United Nations*, Art. 2 no. 4.

4. See Michael Zürn, "'Positives Regieren' jenseits des Nationalstaates. Zur Implementation internationaler Umweltregime" in *Zeitschrift für Internationale Beziehungen*, vol. 4, issue 1 (1997), p. 41 ff.; ibid., *Regieren jenseits des Nationalstaates* (Berlin: Suhrkamp, 1998).

5. Kant, *Perpetual Peace* (First Supplement), http://fs2.american.edu/dfagel/www/Class%20Readings/Kant/Immanuel%20Kant,%20_Perpetual%20Peace_.pdf (accessed December 14, 2020).

6. See the review of the literature in Canh Phuc Nguyen and Christophe Schinckus, "The Spending Behaviour of Government through the Lenses of Global Uncertainty and Economic Integration" in *Journal for Economic Forecasting*, 23 (2020), pp. 35 ff.

7. Rüdiger Safranski, *Wieviel Globalisierung verträgt der Mensch?* (Munich: Fischer, 2019).

8. Lasse Folke Henriksen and Leonard Seabrooke, "Elites in Transnational Policy Networks" in *Global Networks*, 2020, https://doi.org/10.1111/glob.12301 (accessed 11 November 9, 2020).

9. Every kind of political rulership has to justify the improbable asymmetry of command and obedience and also give it a foundation in affect. Such justifications always involve fictions of unity. See Udo Di Fabio, *Herrschaft und Gesellschaft* (Tübingen: Mohr Siebeck, 2019), pp. 22 ff.

10. Klaus Thomalla, *Herrschaft des Gesetzes, Nicht des Menschen* (Tübingen: Mohr Siebeck, 2019), pp. 232 ff.; Georges Goedert, "Die souveräne Gemeinschaft und ihre Untertanen. Zur 'volonté générale' bei Jean-Jacques Rousseau" in *Perspektiven der Philosophie*, Neues Jahrbuch, vol. 38, 2012, pp. 257 ff.

11. Ramashray Roy and Raj Kamal Srivastava, *Dialogues on Development. The Individual, Society and Political Order* (New Delhi: Sage, 1986), p. 97.

12. Kamal Eldin Osman Sali, "The Roots and Causes of the 2011 Arab Uprisings" in *Arab Studies Quarterly*, vol. 35 (2013), pp. 184 ff.

13. Fern Tay Huey, "Hong Kong student 'umbrella revolution' movement takes to social media to separate fact from fiction in pro-democracy protests", ABC News, September 30, 2014, https://www.abc.net.au/news/2014-09-30/feature-social-media-use-in-hong-kong-protests/5780224, (accessed December 7, 2020).

14. Barbara Lippert and Volker Perthes (eds.), "Strategische Rivalität zwischen USA und China" in *SWP Studie* (1) (2020), p. 38. For a somewhat older analysis of China's cultural characteristics in foreign policy, see Jürgen Bellers, *Politische Kultur und Außenpolitik im Vergleich* (Berlin: De Gruyter Oldenbourg, 1999), pp. 42 ff. A similarly older notion that China would gradually abandon its ideological adherences (see for example Hans Helmut Taake, "China: von der ideologischen Fixierung zu außenpolitischem Pragmatismus" in *Entwicklungspolitiken. 33 Geberprofile*, ed. Reinold E. Thiel

(Hamburg, 1996), pp. 233 ff.), would certainly have to be updated, as a new ideology is emerging that points away from Marxism and towards a new form of Sino-nationalism.

15. Hanns W. Maull (ed.), "Auflösung oder Ablösung? Die internationale Ordnung im Umbruch" in *SWP Studie* (2017), p. 21.

16. One does not have to be convinced of the rightness of this notion ("a fools' game"?), to appreciate its effectiveness: Juliette Ringeisen-Biardeaud, "'Let's take back control': Brexit and the Debate on Sovereignty" in *French Journal of British Studies*, XXII-2, (2017).

17. Di Fabio, *Herrschaft und Gesellschaft*, pp. 235 ff.

18. Even in Switzerland, the right is now already discussing a new kind of flexibility: Andrés Payer, "Klimawandel als strafrechtlicher Notstand. Zugleich Besprechung des Urteils des Bezirksgerichts Lausanne" PE19.000742/PCL/llb, January 13, 2020, sui generis 2020, pp. 226 ff.

19. Hasso Hofmann, *Geschichtlichkeit und Universalitätsanspruch des Rechtsstaats* in *Der Staat*, 34 (1995), pp. 1 ff.; Thomalla, *Herrschaft des Gesetzes*, pp. 387 ff.

20. Udo Di Fabio, *Schwankender Westen* (Munich: C.H. Beck, 2015), pp. 137 ff.

CHAPTER 2

LEGITIMACY IN THE NEW WORLD ORDER

STEFAN KORIOTH

I.

A main character in the 2015 novel *Purity*, by the American author Jonathan Franzen is Andreas Wolf, the son of a GDR official who is in charge of the "Sunlight Project," a whistle-blowing website operating from deep within the South American jungle. The platform uses idealistic computer experts to collect and disseminate secret data from governments and defense companies. The goal is to make the world fairer and more transparent. The echoes of WikiLeaks are inescapable. In fact, however, Andreas Wolf also uses violence, money, deception, and manipulation; the claim that his platform is pursuing legitimate interests is questionable. In any event, no one is "pure." What unfolds in the novel as a complex network of relationships in a changing world, in which knowledge from failed surveillance states is used to influence current behavior, can also be read as a serious question about the legitimacy of individual, social, and political action in the current circumstances. As such, the book dramatically illustrates today's uncertainties about what is right or wrong and what is legitimate or illegitimate. Moreover, in just the last 30 years, legitimacy as a key concept of social order has come a long way, and notions of legitimacy have undergone significant changes in their points of reference.

Broadly speaking, legitimacy means the belief of members of a society and those subject to rule or rulership that the rules and goals of coexistence are appropriate and justified. This forms the basis for the validity of a system, especially a political system, and the right to govern. In a narrower sense and as a legal term, legitimacy usually means a positive judgment about the correctness of the state system, including those standards to which every government and every code of conduct must answer. The International Covenant on Civil and Political Rights (1966) includes the people's right of self-determination (Art. 1), free elections (Art. 25), and effective respect for basic human rights (Art. 2) among these standards of legitimacy. Being able to successfully claim legitimacy is a basic requirement for the acceptance of collective decisions and the exercise of political rulership. Everyone involved in politics, not just those in power, has the greatest interest in such legitimacy.

For a long time, the point of reference for legitimacy was the state, an entity usually organized and united according to national principles. Today, by contrast, there are many sources of regulation and rulership—state, non-state, supranational and international, hierarchical and non-hierarchical. What does it mean when legitimacy loses its clear point of reference? How can legitimacy in pluralistic systems be explained and established? Why do many people today think that transnational private organizations such as WikiLeaks (or, in Jonathan Franzen's book, the fictional "Sunlight Project") deserve a greater degree of trust and might have a better claim to legitimacy than governments? The following essay will examine this, looking initially at the development

STEFAN KORIOTH

of notions of legitimation (II.) and subsequently the current requirements of such notions (III.).

II.

In the Middle Ages, legitimacy meant the religious legitimacy of rulership, validated by the acclamation of the subjugated and substantiated by the personal authority of the ruler, and this underpinned the lawfulness of individual decisions. The legitimacy of rulership was a bulwark against usurpers, but it also protected the country and its people against tyranny, because in addition to justifying rulership it also defined its limits. Later on, the absolute ruler was the ruler expressly chosen by the grace of God, whose legitimacy was now dynastic and hereditary, and the source of *majestas*, splendor, and glory. The French Revolution changed everything. Now, for the first time, legitimacy became interrelated with legality—the lawfulness of government actions based on written laws and, above all, written constitutions. The religious and dynastic legitimacy of rulership disappeared. At the Congress of Vienna, European rulers opposed this—one last time and without long-lasting success—invoking the "principle of legitimacy" as justification

44

that, despite the new European order created by Napoleon, the old powers should immediately regain their rights. According to this principle of legitimacy, the Napoleonic wars were in fact just power without legitimation, disrupting historical rights that should now be restored. But it wasn't that easy. After written constitutions had been introduced, monarchical and the constitutional legitimation stood side-by-side until, in the concept of the constitutional state and subsequently the sovereignty of the people, the principle of legality— rulership exercised and limited according to self-determined laws—came to the fore. In the early 20th century, this development was recognized by Max Weber, who made a distinction between traditional, charismatic, and legal rulership. For Weber, legal rulership is the constitutive principle of the modern world—it is legitimized by predetermined, fixed rules, usually in the form of law, which are implemented by a rational bureaucracy. According to Weber's famous definition, what the three types of rulership have in common is that they mean the "chance that specific (or all) commands will be met by obedience on the part of a specifiable group of persons."[1] By contrast with purely factual "power," "rulership" is characterized by "belief in legitimacy."

STEFAN KORIOTH

The modern constitutional state reversed the old principle that legitimacy led to lawfulness. Now the rulership of law, legality, was the origin of legitimacy. "The legislative state," noted Carl Schmitt with a hint of criticism, "is the typical vehicle of a reformist-revisionist era armed with a party program, which attempts to bring about 'progress' through the appropriate statutes passed through legal parliamentary channels." What was now dominant, Schmitt claimed, was the "ethos of the jurisdiction state." "If in this system words like 'legitimacy' and 'authority' are still generally used, then they are only an expression of legality...."[2] Legitimacy should follow from legality—or they may even be identical. In Weimar Republic Germany, however, cracks quickly developed, as Schmitt described. If all aspirations and interests can become the substance of legality, then the "distinctive rationalism of the system of legality is [...] recast into its opposite."[3] The new order that emerged after World War II aimed to prevent arbitrariness. Now the constitution unequivocally turned incontestable issues into norms; the "set of values" described in Germany's Basic Law [*Grundgesetz*, GG] was the expression of this new approach to giving the much extended domain of legality the right to legitimacy.

But that too had its limitations. The first problems became evident in the 1980s when, with the advent of "civil disobedience"—opposition to nuclear power and in the practice of squatting, for example—enhanced entitlements were played off against legality. The granting of "church asylum" to people who, according to the rules of legality, have no right of residence in Germany is also one of these phenomena of the new legitimacy that consciously resists legality and accepts the sanctions that are applied as a result. The state reacted only occasionally with a strict enforcement of legality, as in a current example against "Reich Citizens" [*Reichsbürger*] who completely reject the legality and legitimacy of the existing system. Much more frequently, the state tried to find solutions through negotiation, communication, and concessions, with sometimes less and sometimes more skill and success. The Leviathan of legitimacy was turned first into a tamed Leviathan then into a useful pet.[4]

III.

It is, however, not only in the case of such domestic social conflicts and here of its own free will that the state has become a manager of rulership whose legitimacy is under attack. In completely different domains, globalization and internationalization have ousted the state, forcing states with a monopoly of rulership to compete with supranational and international organizations as well as non-governmental organizations (NGOs) and companies. How can legitimacy be established in light of these imbrications, i.e. in the spirit of Max Weber, the belief that the rules that now come from multiple sources are appropriate and justified? We must first make some distinctions. A group of the aforementioned intergovernmental organizations, such as the European Union and the United Nations in particular, originate in states that, as members of the club, determine such organizations' tasks, duties, powers, and funding. Here, legitimacy can be derived from the members, as difficult as it may be in individual cases. This also applies to transnational organizations with a limited range of tasks that can, however, be extremely important, such as in the case of the World Trade Organization, the World Bank, and the International Monetary Fund.

The second group that is becoming increasingly important both quantitatively and qualitatively comprises global governance institutions in a broad sense. They are completely independent of states and international communities. These include NGOs, importantly, environmental groups such as Greenpeace or critics of capitalism such as Attac, but also spontaneous groups like the Fridays for Future movement, global foundations and multinational companies, who have control over and an oligopoly of the supply of generally required goods, especially digital services. In the wake of the financial crisis of 2008/09, law firms were also the source of much debate, as they drafted and wrote the regulations—sometimes even on behalf of state legislators—to which the financial institutions they advised should then be committed. All these very different groups claim a legitimacy derived from their self-imposed task, whether it be derived from moral authority, expertise, or the critical oversight of pressing issues such as energy supply or environmental protection in civil society. On closer inspection, however, many of them often also pursue special interests with the risk that better organized and better financed interests will have a stronger voice and are more likely to succeed.

It goes without saying that such groups, companies, and associations can represent and take up particular rights like any group, but this is not the crucial point. They want more public legitimacy, with, alongside, or against the state. To deny them this from the outset would correspond to the classic view of international and constitutional law, which sees the common good as residing in states and associations of states, but does not solve any of the pressing problems and attempts to ignore what is going on now. Counting in their favor, most of the new competitors for legitimacy are innovative and can inject new ideas into the global discourse more quickly than slow-moving public institutions. Formal and issue-related criteria that can grant legitimacy to these groups under certain circumstances are therefore central. The formal standards are participation and transparency, which enable codetermination and control and thus create the trust that is indispensable for legitimacy. Participation requires that those who are directly or indirectly affected by such organizations must be given the opportunity to participate, while transparency requires the disclosure of decision-making processes and financial sources. By submitting to supervisory bodies, the group's actions must be open to a review of legality. Internal controls and legality reviews, including private jurisdiction in the form of arbitration courts such as in international sports federations, can only have a limited scope and cannot replace state and international courts. Absolute limits to the freedom of action of state-independent groups exist when the application of legal constraints and the competence to make generally binding legislation are an issue. In terms of issues, such groups can only claim legitimacy if they are focused on the common good—an aspect which is also subject to review. In this, it is likely that a diversity of opinions will lead to fragmentation when it comes to deciding what is or should be done when dealing with crises in all spheres of life.

All of these requirements have today turned out to be very practical on several occasions. For example, Germany's Environmental Appeals Act (UmwRG) also deals with the question of the conditions under which private groups—representatives, as it were, of the common good alongside (and against) the state—can bring legal action against state measures in the environmental domain.[5] In a specific individual case, the Federal Fiscal Court, as the highest court in financial matters, refused to recognize Attac, a group critical of capitalism, as non-profit in the eyes of tax law; a general political orientation, combined with "dramatic means of expression", is not enough: "Anyone who pursues political purposes by influencing political decision-making and shaping public opinion does not fulfill a charitable purpose" according to the Federal Fiscal Court. Political activity and "education take[s] place in intellectual openness. It cannot be funded if it is used to influence political decision-making and public opinion in terms of its own views."[6] We should note, however, that this is not about the undisputed fundamental rights to freedom and legitimacy to exert political influence and express one's own views as forcefully as possible in public discourse, but solely about whether the state must or can give tax advantages to particular opinions.

Models for the allocation and delimitation of state and non-state sources of legitimacy are not entirely new. In some ways they are reminiscent of the centuries-old cooperation and conflict between the state and the Churches, in which the latter also claimed a public mission and an orientation towards the common good. In this case, the solution in many jurisdictions consists in expressly granting to religious communities autonomy in their own affairs alongside the basic right of religious freedom, but this does not exempt them from observing the generally applicable law.[7] However, this parallel also reveals the problems of transferring such an approach to autonomy to global governance institutions. It would need the formation of a world state in order to grant global NGOs autonomy that can be monitored and to establish effective boundaries. However, such a world state, just like a "subsidiary form of world organization," a "subsidiary world republic" (in the words of Otfried Höffe), will remain a utopia. In addition to the thinking in spheres outlined above, it is therefore advisable to pursue another approach, one which was developed by Michel Foucault as early as the 1980s, at that time related solely to domestic processes.[8] In questions of legitimacy, Foucault recommended proceeding not from institutions, but from the activities of governing, planning, and shaping. "Governmentality," he said, is an information-based configuration of life experiences that by no means has to be state-centered, but rather has to take into account all relationships of power and influence. That was insightful, because in the age of global legitimacy it really comes down to communication and the coordination of different interests and sources of legitimacy. But still—and this problem remains: who makes the rules? States in their current form will play their part when they notice a change: "In the emerging global society, the hierarchical legal model of western legal cultures is undergoing a mutation that is turning it into 'something else'."[9] Ultimately, perhaps a horizontally structured, global law will emerge from various sources.

Notes

1. Max Weber, *Economy and Society*, ed. and trans. Keith Tribe (Cambridge MA: University of Harvard Press, 2019), p. 338.

2. Carl Schmitt, *Legality and Legitimacy*, trans. and ed. Jeffrey Seitzer, (Durham NC and London: Duke University Press, 2004), pp. 8–9.

3. Schmitt, *Legality*, p. 10.

4. Erhard Denninger, *Der gebändigte Leviathan* (Nomos: Baden-Baden 1990), p. 29.

5. The law says (§ 3 UmwRG) that this is possible if the environmental association pursues goals related to the common good, is recognized as charitable in terms of tax law, and its internal structure is democratic.

6. BFH, NJW 2019, 877 (Judgment of January 10, 2019, V R 60/17).

7. In Germany Art. 140 GG / Art. 137 Para. 3 WRV (Weimar Constitution).

8. Michel Foucault, *Security, Territory, Population: Lectures at the Collège de France*, ed. Arnold I. Davidson, trans. Graham Burchell (London: Palgrave Macmillan, 2007).

9. Marc Amstutz and Vagios Karavas, "Rechtsmutation: Zu Genese und Evolution des Rechts im transnationalen Raum" in *Rechtsgeschichte*, 9 (2006), p. 14 ff., 15.

CHAPTER 3

OUR GLOBAL LEGITIMACY CRISIS

MAHA HOSAIN AZIZ

My work over the last decade has focused on risk, which basically means identifying the threats to our stability—what could go wrong. Originally, I focused on country-specific risk, looking at individual countries and what would make these countries tick. After doing that for a few years, I started to see that the risks in one part of the world and one country were comparable to the risks in other regions and other countries around the world. It led me to this larger thesis about our global legitimacy crisis. I realized during this risk-focused exploration in the 2010s that the same sorts of issues were coming up in every type of context, every political context, every economic context, and so forth.

There are of course critics of such ideas and this qualitative, risk-focused approach. People in my field are sometimes criticized for the predictions we make about risk. Some people say that we're not held accountable when we're wrong. In fact, they even go so far as to say that "human beings who spend their lives studying the state of the world are poorer forecasters than dart-throwing monkeys!" Of course, nobody can predict what is coming with 100 percent accuracy, but at the very least I want to take this opportunity to share my risk-focused view of the world—a global legitimacy crisis that defined the 2010s and is likely to deepen in the 2020s in our pandemic world, even in a post-Trump era. Certain perceived norms were challenged in four key areas in the last decade—in our geopolitics, our politics, our economies, and our societies—and this will likely continue during this decade.

Geopolitically, we have been at a crossroads for a while. There's a tendency to over-emphasize former US President Donald Trump and his role in pushing the world away from a US-led international system during his term. The reality is we were questioning US hegemony for over a decade, long before President Trump took office. It is of course encouraging that someone with (a decent character and) a democratic vision—President Joe Biden—now governs the US. He talks about the US leading the world again. But we have to consider if the world, beyond America's traditional Western allies, actually wants the US to lead. President Biden's globalist policy vision does not necessarily mean everything will just snap back into place, or that US leadership will be accepted by all actors in the international community. A lot has changed in the last few years. Certain powers have risen and certain forces have been unleashed.

The post-Cold War era led by the US and a US-led international community is still largely behind us. There are multiple examples from the 2010s that showed this was the case. But this begs the question: what is the world order in the 2020s? In his book *Has China Won?*, Kishore Mahbubani writes about how the world is being defined by the US-versus-China dynamic—and that China has the edge longer term. Is that competition going to shape this decade as opposed to a US hegemonic system? Or is our future geopolitical order simply Asian in terms of the rise of China and other actors in that region, as Parag Khanna argues in his book *The Future Is Asian*? We may also revisit the idea of multipolarity, with different superpowers dominating in different parts of the world on different issues. But a better way to understand the world right now and for the coming decade is that it's simply post-hegemonic. We know the US had a different role under President Trump, and his anti-globalist legacy may hinder President Biden's ability to truly unite a fractured world.

What is even more interesting to note is the rise of non-state actors in the last decade. As our governments have muddled through geopolitically, we have seen citizens armed with tech in every part of the world show that they are a force to be reckoned with on a global stage. For instance, they are reacting to global issues—consider Greta Thunberg and other teenagers around the world who are leading the charge against climate change in response to a lack of global leadership on this issue. We saw waves of protest around the world in reaction to some of President Trump's policies—immigration, the travel ban, women's rights, and so on. In order to understand the way the world order is evolving, we must take into account the rise of the non-state actor, i.e. the tech-armed citizen protester. Related to that, we also cannot deny the growing role played by activist billionaires, especially activist tech billionaires. I don't just mean people like Bill Gates who has been around for a while. There's been a wave of other tech billionaires like Jack Ma, Jack Dorsey, and

Elon Musk in the last decade, who seem to be talking about policy and global issues in a public space much more than we've seen in the past. They are political influencers stepping up to fill a perceived gap in global leadership.

The point we must reflect on is that the nature of power on a global stage may be evolving. It's not sufficient to simply look at the world through a state-centric lens or to simply discuss who is the superpower and who is not. One could even argue that some tech firms have more power than most governments in some ways. As our definition of power changes, we are also not going to be clear who's in charge in the 2020s, just as it wasn't clear in the 2010s. We won't have a consensus on the structure of the world order. That is part of our geopolitical legitimacy crisis.

Politically, it's safe to say that pre-COVID-19, the last decade has shown us that citizens in many different types of political contexts are just not happy with their governments or the political status quo. In many academic and even some policy circles, we've started to question whether democracy is still the best system for us. Will this change in the 2020s? Let's remember there hasn't been a US-led world order or post-Cold War era for a while, in which there's a global consensus about promoting democracy and related values.

Nevertheless, we've been in the midst of a political legitimacy crisis for a while—what I call a "global spring" of anti-government protests not just in the Arab Spring region but across Europe, Latin America, parts of Asia, and of course in the US. There seems to be a recurring feeling among citizens that there simply must be a better way to govern. There must be a better political system. This phenomenon defined the 2010s and will likely continue in the 2020s. Maybe democracy is not the end of history, as Francis Fukuyama had argued at the end of the Cold War.

The question is, what's next? I don't think we can label or define a new political system quite yet. The political system is evolving. We have other types of actors—for example, the citizen protester—trying to fill the gap left by government. We even have non-state actors like the activist billionaire filling the policy gap when governments fall short in places like the US, Nigeria, and Hong Kong. Perhaps in the coming years there will need to be more discussion about a new social contract, including a role for other types of actors. What is it that we expect of our governments, and vice versa?

If we don't do this, we can expect that more citizens will be taking to the streets to challenge and even bring down their leaders and governments. In fact, the last decade has seen politicians slapped in countries like Nepal and Australia. In India and the Maldives, we've seen them being attacked with food. We've observed massive protest movements that have routed or ousted certain world leaders—for example, in Brazil and South Korea—because of corruption. There's clearly a need to look ahead and think about a social contract that reflects our tech-driven society and takes into account these other influencers.

Also, there are multiple studies that reveal that in the US and Europe the younger generation apparently doesn't seem to care as much about democracy.[1] In fact, the Global Peace Index suggests that in the last decade the number of riots has gone up by 282 percent and strikes have gone up by 821 percent.[2] There's clearly a desire on the part of the citizen for something different. This political aspect is definitely part of our global legitimacy crisis. We're at a crossroads in terms of what we want and what we expect from our governments.

Economically, we're all aware that globalization has been challenged by economic nationalism and populism. Going back to 1999, we saw citizens protesting about the perceived inequality arising from globalization. In the 2010s, we witnessed a state-led challenge from certain politicians embracing populism as a counter to globalization. But the point I want to emphasize is that we will need to reflect more on our relationship with our work. It's no secret—activist tech billionaires have been warning us in the last decade and they'll continue to warn us—that 40 percent of us will likely lose our jobs because of automation in the next 10 to 15 years. Of course, this was said in a pre-COVID-19 context. The question is: what will happen to those individuals who are left behind not just by globalization or the previous global youth unemployment crisis but also because of automation?

It's important to be aware of this concept called the precariat coined by economist Guy Standing.[3] It's an emergent social class—those who have been left behind by these different phenomena. They are in a precarious position because they have perhaps moved from one temporary job to another and have not been able to develop an occupational identity as a result.

One could argue that this lack of occupational identity bleeds into a mental health crisis. It's worth reflecting on the fact that our relationship with our work is going to change. We've been warned multiple times by techies that we need to do something about that. Who are we in relation to our work? Could there be a need to redefine the moral economy or the economic contract that we have with our governments?

Lastly, there is the social aspect of our global legitimacy crisis. We are all aware that in the last decade we've seen the rise of hate not just within society but also at the level of the state and some political parties. The rise of xenophobia is something that we can't ignore. The fact that there's no counter-narrative to the hate is something that we must be aware of.

I think the only world leader who has truly talked about this issue in a pre-COVID-19 world is New Zealand's Prime Minister Jacinda Ardern. After the attacks in Christchurch in 2019, she called for a global campaign against hate and extremism. We need to have a larger discussion about what our shared global values are. We didn't have that debate in the 2010s. Can we have it in the 2020s? That will be important if we want to redefine our values and our identity within our countries and as a global community.

These are the elements of our global legitimacy crisis. We're at a turning point in these four key areas. And it is likely that this global legitimacy crisis will deepen in the 2020s, even in a post-Trump era.

But then COVID-19 happened. I think the COVID-19 effect on our global legitimacy crisis shows that the era of US-led multilateralism is dead. It's encouraging that the G7 and the G20 met virtually to discuss a global response, but I think we can agree that there's been a lack of coordination in dealing with this common threat. It's encouraging that UK Prime Minister Boris Johnson talks about introducing a D10, another new type of advisory body for leading democracies, and President Biden is spearheading a Global Summit for Democracy. But what is more relevant for understanding the effect of COVID-19 on geopolitics is the emergence of a COVID-19 bilateralism.

China has taken a big role in sending medical supplies and masks around the world as we've dealt with the pandemic in different countries globally. We've also seen countries like Turkey and Cuba send doctors in a form of COVID-19 bilateralism, which more appropriately captures our current world order. How will these bilateral relationships evolve? How will they impact stability? That's a big question mark; we'll have to wait and see. It's also worth recognizing another form of COVID-19 bilateralism—state to non-state. It involves the activist billionaires from the US and China engaging directly with governments to offer COVID-19-related support. How will that dynamic reshape power or the world order as we know it in the coming decade? That's what we need to think about.

The COVID-19 effect on our geopolitics is clearly negative. But this is also an opportunity for us to come up with new ideas. How do we want the world order to evolve if traditional institutions are not working and lack legitimacy? Are there other ways we can think about the world? Well, one suggestion is what if we had a new G7-like advisory body with leaders who are beating the virus and are taking the lead? It just so happens that most of the leaders who've had success are women. Maybe we need a female G7-like advisory body guiding us through these sorts of global challenges.

Second, the COVID-19 effect on our political legitimacy crisis is significant. I'm a global citizen with Pakistani roots. I live in New York and I have strong ties to London, but when the pandemic happened I was hanging on the words of President Trump and Prime Minister Johnson during their press conferences, hoping that they would come up with a solution for what we were dealing with early on. I was ready to believe in them.

I think there was a brief time when governments could regain the legitimacy that they had lost in the previous decade, but over time perceptions have changed and now people often think that governments are falling short. We've seen waves of protest in the UK, the US, India, and in other parts of the world. So we can expect that the legitimacy crisis that many governments have faced is going to be renewed as time goes on and as we as citizens ask "Did they do enough? Did so many people need to die?"

As already mentioned, one solution would be to renew or to redefine the social contract. What do we expect of our governments at this stage in a COVID-19 world? Again, why don't we have more female leaders in government, since so far they've had more success relative to their male counterparts? Also, given the role of activist billionaires, not just in terms of philanthropy but suggesting policy in the COVID-19 context—everyone from Elon Musk to Jack Ma to Adrian Cheng and of course Bill Gates—is this the time to think about a more defined role for the activist billionaire in the social contract or political context? Obviously, this is controversial because they're not elected. But we need to recognize that the new influencers are trying to fill the gap left by government. A group of 85 millionaires, the "Millionaires for Humanity," have signed a pledge saying philanthropy is not enough. They're calling on governments to tax them more to help us ease out of this massive crisis. Clearly there are other types of actors that are coming up with policy prescriptions. Again, do we need a new social contract for a COVID-19 world?

Third, we all know that most governments have come up with economic relief packages. It sounded very encouraging in the beginning, but finance ministers around the world have said that not everybody can be helped. That will of course contribute to more precariats who will feel they've been left behind and have fallen through the cracks. This will potentially bleed deeper into a larger mental health crisis.

I suggest we think about a moral economy, an updated economic contract with our governments. What is it that we expect? What's the minimum we can expect from our governments in the COVID-19 context? And one more female-oriented point: isn't this the time to ensure or advance gender equality? According to one McKinsey study, that would add about $12 trillion to global growth.[4] These are the sorts of ideas we can think about. There has also been a recurrent debate about basic income. Should that be something we can offer those who have been hit hardest by COVID-19?

Lastly, there has been a COVID-19 effect on society. Initially and in theory, COVID-19 brought us together; we were all united against this shared enemy. We all had, and continue to have, a shared goal—we want to live. That's obviously positive. But we also saw quite a few cases of hate in the context of this pandemic, for instance there has been an East-Asian backlash in the US and parts of Europe because of the perceived origins of the virus. We've also seen COVID-related misinformation campaigns in India and Malaysia targeting Muslims.

The existing risk or threat to our stability involving identity issues has been exacerbated. But there is a silver lining to the pandemic in that it gave us an opportunity to see that there is one other shared global value—this came as a result of the George Floyd event in May 2020 in the US. It's remarkable to have witnessed that citizens in the midst of a global pandemic felt they should protest on the streets against racism and hate in all 50 US states and in over 60 countries around the world. It shows that there is indeed a sense of shared global values or global community united around anti-racism. And it's being led by citizens, not by our governments. We need to have more discussions and debates about what our shared global values are in a COVID-19 world and beyond.

This is my vision for the world through the lens of global risk. This is a global legitimacy crisis that took shape in the 2010s and which will likely deepen in the 2020s, with the pandemic cloud hovering over us and even with a more traditional US leadership at the helm.

Notes

1. See for example Stefan Foa and Yascha Mounk, "The Signs of Deconsolidation" in *Journal of Democracy* 28 (2017), pp. 5–15.

2. Institute for Economics & Peace, "Global Peace Index 2020: Measuring Peace in a Complex World," June 2020, p. 2. https://visionofhumanity.org/wp-content/uploads/2020/10/GPI_2020_web.pdf (accessed November 24, 2020).

3. Guy Standing, *The Precariat: The New Dangerous Class* (London: Bloomsbury Academic, 2016).

4. McKinsey Global Institute, "The Power of Parity: How Advancing Women's Equality Can Add $12 Trillion to Global Growth," September 2017. https://www.mckinsey.com/featured-insights/employment-and-growth/how-advancing-womens-equality-can-add-12-trillion-to-global-growth (accessed November 16, 2020).

CHAPTER 4

WHAT IS THE SOURCE OF LEGITIMACY FOR NGOs AND OTHER ACTORS IN CIVIL SOCIETY?

RUDOLF MELLINGHOFF

INTRODUCTION

When dealing with new, present-day constellations, changes to existing institutions, and the legitimacy of national and global actors, forms of action, and institutions, we must also examine the involvement of citizens in non-governmental organizations (NGOs), citizens' initiatives, interest groups, non-profit organizations, clubs, foundations, and associations. In the wake of globalization, the international network of NGOs involved in the areas of environmental protection, social justice, and human rights has become increasingly important. Between the early 1990s and 2015, the number of NGOs almost doubled.[1] NGOs operate as lobbyists, taking part in international negotiations to develop global standards and norms, or acting as service providers and experts in the provision of monitoring, coordination, and consultancy. The example of "Fridays for Future" clearly shows how a credible social movement of schoolchildren and students can quickly develop into a globally significant movement, winning over large sections of the population, changing the behavior of governments, and leading to the creation of numerous support organizations.

In Germany and the globalized world, civic engagement is diverse. In parliamentary democracies, the question of democratic legitimacy arises particularly in those cases where associations, clubs, or other civil society organizations exert a direct influence on politics and parliamentary decision-making, and claim to speak for a large majority of the population. This essay aims to contribute merely a few—necessarily fragmentary— thoughts on an issue on which a myriad publications and essays already exist.

1. CIVIC ENGAGEMENT

The postwar models of liberal democracy were characterized by a comparatively stable system in which interests were mediated via political parties, associations, and trade unions. These bodies performed an essential function promoting integration within society as well as preventing the gap between citizens and political decision-makers from becoming too great. Even though these institutions still exist today, we cannot ignore the fact that over the course of time they have at least in part lost their formative power, their traditional force, and their influence over political events. People are talking about a crisis in democratic institutions and a disintegration of the postwar model of representation. It is claimed that this crisis, which may also be a crisis of capitalism, has led to new forms of participation.[2]

Over time, numerous organizations, movements, and forms of action have emerged that are influencing the political structure of the community. These were and are described using the terms "third sector," "non-governmental organizations (NGOs)," "non-profit organizations (NPOs)," or other forms of activity in civil society. At least since the beginning of the 1990s, these diverse activities, forms of action, and organizations have been amalgamated under the umbrella term "civil society." Civic engagement is regarded as an indispensable basis for social cohesion.[3]

Forms of action in civil society can be traced back to antiquity. In the English-speaking legal world, "civil society" is an integral part of the description of organizations, bodies, and movements that influence politics. Nonetheless, the concept and manifestations of civil society remain comparatively vague and undefined.[4] In many cases, civil society is classified as a third sector alongside the state and economy (or market). Others describe it as the space between the state, the economy, and the private sphere or family. In some cases, civil society is even positively recast as the totality of public associations, bodies, movements, and groups where citizens meet on a voluntary basis, and includes within the concept of civil society not just established organizations, but also unaffiliated engagement in the context of demonstrations, strikes, petitions, boycotts, or other forms of action. By contrast, political science only counts civic engagement via organizations, but not unorganized people as individuals, as part of civil society. In the debate about civil society, a distinction can also be made between more neutral, open descriptions and judgmental definitions. On the one hand, the distinction between the state and the economy or market, as well as privacy and family is seen as sufficient. Other concepts focus on moral values such as non-violence, self-organization, self-sufficiency, or other republican, democratic virtues, require a utopian aspect, and exclude, for example, charitable foundations from the definition.

In a guide for elected officials, political advisors, the media, and interested citizens, the political scientist and historian Robert Graf Strachwitz defines civil society rather broadly.[5] By civil society, he understands movements, organizations, and institutions as well as numerous unorganized or spontaneous collective actions that are set up on a voluntary basis, pursue subjective goals of the common good, and do not carry out any state—in the sense of sovereign—responsibilities. They are not geared towards making a profit and do not distribute surpluses from their activities to members, shareholders, or third parties; they act in a self-empowered and self-organized manner, and are largely dependent on gifts such as empathy and time as well as the material resources of others. Depending on their function, civil society organizations can be divided into services, advocacy, custodians, mediators, self-help groups, community-building, political participation, or personal fulfillment. They can support government action, separate themselves from society, or make their voices heard. They can be organized in an associative manner, such as clubs, embody affiliated organizations, such as foundations, or exist as societies—organizations that are owned by external parties. Their goals are extremely diverse and can relate to welfare, research, education and training, culture, nature and environmental protection, sport, human and civil rights, religion, and other aims. This demonstrates that the phenomenon of civil society is extremely broad, while the empirical basis of knowledge about civil society remains limited. Civil society organizations are not obliged to provide information to the public or publish reports. Official statistics are often incomplete. There are no binding guidelines for the preparation of accounts or the valuation of assets.

Over the course of globalization, civil society organizations have increasingly organized themselves on an international basis. For example, they espouse human rights, they fight against corruption or for environmental protection. In this context we could mention, among others, world-famous organizations such as Doctors Without Borders, Attac, Amnesty International, Bread for the World, Greenpeace, Human Rights Watch, International Red Cross, Terre des Hommes, Transparency International (TI), World Wide Fund for Nature (WWF), and most recently

Fridays for Future. These bodies operate globally and lobby for the common good. They take part in international political decision-making processes and help set standards and norms. Numerous organizations are also involved at the social level, such as in the fight against poverty and hunger, and provide goods and expertise. Many of these civil society organizations are recognized, respected, and have achieved high accolades worldwide.[6]

However, globally active civil society organizations encounter resistance and are increasingly and in some cases significantly prevented from going about their business or even banned from operating, especially in totalitarian states. In political debate, critics claim that there is a clear north–south divide among such actors, which leads to a political preponderance of developed countries on the international stage, conveying a western worldview, and characterized by universalism, individualism, consumption, and cost–benefit rationality. An independent, critical civil society is opposed by many governments in Africa, Asia, Latin America, and the Middle East. Their freedom of assembly, association, information, and expression is restricted, and they are often monitored, intimidated, defamed, or banned. For some years, the limitation of their scope of action by so-called "NGO laws" has assumed new dimensions.[7] These laws aim to record cash flows and restrict operations through registration and reporting obligations or by banning the organization entirely. Since numerous civil society organizations receive financial resources or donations directly or indirectly from foreign donors, the aim of the NGO laws is to use the state to control such support or cut off domestic initiatives from foreign donations. Political activities of civil society organizations, in particular, are regarded as improper interference, especially if they are financed from abroad. In many cases, states invoke the sovereignty of their own country, especially in order to avoid compromising the political and economic power of the government in question. Today, restrictive NGO laws exist in over 60 countries. They are supplemented by security laws, anti-terror laws, and media laws, which always lead to a more or less extensive restriction of the ability of civil society actors to operate.

Many countries used as a model the 2012 Russian NGO law, which obliges all organizations that receive money from abroad and are politically active to register as "foreign agents."[8] As many organizations did not comply with this, the law was tightened such that the state can even register an organization against its will and, if necessary, declare it to be "undesirable." The latest, 2020 draft of the law narrows the scope of these organizations further by requiring "foreign agents" to inform the Justice Ministry of any planned programs and events, which may then be banned. In addition, there is the option of dissolving the organization in question and classifying individuals as "agents."[9] India has passed an NGO law, according to which all organizations that receive money from abroad must apply for a license, on condition that no political work may be financed using this money. The Egyptian NGO law made it possible to arrest employees who received funds from abroad. After interventions by the UN Human Rights Council, the EU and the United States, the law was made less stringent. However, under the new law, authorities can still crack down on NGO employees.[10] Israel also stipulates in its 2016 NGO law that all organizations receiving more than half of their money from abroad must report this and identify themselves as such to parliament. Even in Europe similar efforts were made. Hungary's Transparency Law stipulated that all organizations receiving donations from abroad had to register with the Hungarian authorities if such donations were above a certain amount, and state that they were "an organization supported from abroad." The Court of Justice of the European Union regarded this as a violation of European law.[11]

2. LEGITIMACY OF CIVIL SOCIETY ORGANIZATIONS

The heterogeneity of civil society organizations and the way they operate makes it hard to establish generally binding rules for activities in civil society. Even if the important role of civil society is a subject for debate almost everywhere today, the term nevertheless encompasses a wide variety of phenomena. It can concern very old, traditional institutions that have been recognized for many years. But civic engagement can also be merely temporary, isolated, and locally limited. As in politics, the priorities of civic engagement are changing, as can be seen from the examples of the peace movement of the 1960s, the anti-nuclear power movement, and the Occupy movement. Applying moral and normative criteria, civic engagement cannot necessarily be viewed as superior, of greater value, or "good." It includes highly commendable forms of social engagement, advocacy for human rights, and the fight against corruption, as well as highly problematic groups like Pegida, the Identitarian Movement, and radical contrarians such as the "Querdenker" movement.

At the international level in particular, however, we can see that since the 1990s civil society organizations have become important actors. While originally NGOs either had no or only a basic right to participate in UN negotiations, today they have extensive opportunities at the UN and its subsidiary bodies, opportunities that are generally not specifically regulated at international level. As a rule, civil society organizations are not granted a comprehensive right to participate in negotiations as a voting member. However, civil society participation in international negotiations and debates is now widely recognized.[12] The United Nations General Assembly broadly supports civil society participation in various policy areas: the respective secretariats and their chairperson then decide on the scope of these privileges. Today, civil society organizations are granted more than a right to be present: they have the opportunity of participating actively in substantive discussions on the formulation of binding agreements, of giving speeches, and of representing their specific positions independently. In most of the subsidiary bodies of the United Nations, the extensive participation of NGOs and others is also a matter of course today. At the supranational level, the participation of civil society in the political process is even specifically regulated. Art. 11 (2) of the EU Treaty provides that the EU institutions maintain an open, transparent, and regular dialogue with representative associations and civil society.[13] This provision was made more specific by the introduction of a regulation on a European citizens' initiative, a direct democratic procedure at European level.[14] At national level, the engagement of civil society in the legislative process is also well advanced. The state governments of Baden-Württemberg and Rhineland-Palatinate have introduced initial forms of public participation. This enables citizens to take part in the creation of state laws via a participation portal.[15] At federal level, too, consultation with civil society in the legislative process is now a matter of course. The Bundestag is also considering new forms of democratic citizen participation.[16]

The participation of civil society organizations in political decision-making processes and, in particular, the involvement of globally active NGOs on an international and supranational level raises the question of their legitimacy. What is the basis of their claim to be involved in global and international negotiations?[17] Participation in political decision-making processes may well come under critical scrutiny. This is especially true bearing in mind that many civil society organizations refer less to their members than to humanity, the citizens of a country, or the silent majority, when they are included in political decision-making processes. They appear as an advocate for the natural world or as a representative of humanity, without it having been established beforehand whether their demands correspond to the needs and wishes of the population. Equally there is no guarantee that the organizations in question will be selected and included in a representative manner. For this reason, it is not uncommon for reference to be made to the serious democratic deficits of transnational and international institutions and procedures as well as to the risks involved in the instrumentalization and collaboration of civil society organizations.[18]

The question of the legitimacy of civil society organizations in political policy-making and decision-making depends essentially on what is meant by legitimacy. The term alone is multifaceted and is defined differently in various disciplines such as political science, philosophy, sociology, and jurisprudence.[19] Historically speaking, the fundamental idea of political legitimacy has changed over time.[20] For example, in the Middle Ages God and tradition were the typical sources of authority. Later, the theory of the social contract as a form of political governance developed. In the 18th and 19th centuries people focused on popular sovereignty; democratic theories of legitimacy developed in the 19th and 20th centuries. In the late 1990s, globalization led to new ideas about the legitimacy of democratic processes, participation, and the legitimacy of international decision-making. Alongside the historical dimension, one can also focus on different concepts.[21] One could, for example, make a distinction between normative and sociological legitimacy, as well as legitimacy through procedures, input legitimacy, or output legitimacy. Depending on whether a more formal and normative understanding is taken as the basis, or whether a participatory understanding of legitimacy or one based on the principle of usefulness forms the starting point, this can lead to different results when answering our initial question.

In constitutional law, the question of democratic legitimacy is raised in order to guarantee the people's influence over the exercise of state authority. This is based on the fact that the people are the bearers and holders of state authority. If Art. 20 (2) (1) of the German Basic Law prescribes that all state authority is derived from the people, only those decisions that can be based on the will of the people are democratically legitimate. A distinction is made between functional, organizational/personnel, and factual/substantive legitimacy.[22] The aim of these different forms of legitimacy is to bring about and ensure the effective influence of the people on the exercise of state authority. In terms of organization and personnel, democratic legitimacy exists if the officials entrusted with observing state affairs can rely on an uninterrupted chain of legitimacy that can be traced back to the people. In this way, the state institutions in which and for which the officials act are democratically legitimized. Both an indirect and a direct legitimacy created by the people is permissible. Substantively too, the exercise of state authority must be based on the will of the people. The same idea underlies the unitarian legitimacy model or input legitimacy, according to which the democratic principle is institutionally implemented only by actors legitimized by elections. Since civil society organizations or actors are not able to rely on such an act of legitimacy, their participation in the decision-making process is regarded critically. Such inadequate legitimacy is highlighted not only at the national level, but also in the international decision-making process.[23] From a democratic point of view, the participation of civil society actors might even be viewed as problematic because it threatens to weaken the relevant context of legitimacy.[24] Accordingly, for decision-making in international politics, from a procedural perspective only the representatives sent by the national governments enjoy sufficient democratic legitimacy. If one wanted to strengthen the democratic legitimacy of the decisions of international organizations, the route would have to lead via the respective national parliaments, which control what governments do at an international level and what measures they agree to. It is argued, furthermore, that the participation of civil society cannot be organized procedurally in such a way that meets democratic requirements, and there is only one concept of democratic legitimacy that applies at both state and international/supranational level.[25] Such democratic legitimacy would require the equal participation of all those governed in the exercise of sovereign authority.[26] Of course, even in these circumstances, it might not be problematic to consult civil society organizations in connection with the emergence of laws, international agreements, or comparable regulations. However, direct participation in the decision-making process itself would contradict democratic legitimacy.

On the other hand, in political science in particular, we have seen the increasing significance of models of legitimacy that are connected with the necessity for citizens to participate in the political process or become functionally useful in society. In this context, the concepts of output legitimacy and participatory democracy theories are particularly important. For example, output legitimacy is not linked to procedural requirements for the establishment of norms, but to the results of legislation and thus to the content of a regulation. It matters less whether democratically legitimized officials are responsible for the regulations. Rather, it is crucial that they are accepted by the subjects of the laws, that they comply with fundamental norms such as international human rights, and that they conform to the rules of good legislation. The participation of civil society would lead to better regulations because they would be based on a broader decision-making foundation and a better basis of information.

In particular, the concept of democracy through participation gives civil society legitimacy for its actions when participating in national and international regulations. Based on the consideration that there is a democratic deficit and a lack of opportunities for participation in the existing representative democracies, participation is considered necessary, especially by those particularly affected by decision-making. This is intended to compensate for possible democratic deficits and to take better account of the citizens' views. At the same time, participation by civil society leads to more transparency; this makes decisions more comprehensible and more accountable. In international law, the participation of civil society is discussed under the concept of the pluralistic model of legitimacy.[27] The participation of NGOs as part of an international civil society is intended to increase the democratic content of decisions at international level. Civil society organizations and actors introduce citizens' essential demands into the process if they are involved in the decision-making process. As an important, positive effect, we should emphasize that the international public realm related with this creates an indispensable transparency in international politics. To this extent, there is a close connection with so-called deliberative democracy, which emphasizes public debate including citizens' participation in and influence on the decision-making process.

CONCLUDING REMARKS

Despite a number of concerns and objections, civil society organizations play an important and now generally recognized role in the political process. First and foremost, it is not about the decision-making responsibility for particular regulations, but about participating in the creation of national, international, and supranational decisions. Ideally, participation leads to decisions that are better because they are based on a better background of information, and thus to the acceptability of measures and regulations. Civil society organizations therefore comprise some of the key players in policy-making today. They uncover grievances, raise important issues such as environmental protection, social justice, and human rights, and ensure that the social and ecological consequences of human action are taken into account. The participation of civil society organizations and actors in the political decision-making process creates a public realm that counteracts the risk of powerful interest groups exerting a one-sided influence. Civil society can introduce new topics and previously neglected issues into the debate. International organizations whose procedures are mainly based on traditional, cumbersome institutions that are largely limited to the nation state, need the important complement of organized civil society. The latter helps ensure that citizens' concerns and interests can be articulated directly at international level. By contrast with democratically legitimized states, civil society organizations are not restricted to seeking the greatest possible consensus and balance between various interests. Due to their intensive focus on a particular issue, they can introduce into the political debate important aspects that are not weakened by numerous agreements and considerations. It is then up to the respective decision-makers to consider and weigh the arguments, contributions, and viewpoints.

Civil society organizations can draw on knowledge and resources in many areas that are often superior to those of other participants in the decision-making process. This justifies involving them in the political process, including them in negotiations and deliberations, and taking their demands seriously. The shortcomings of civil society, which are sometimes considerable, should not be overlooked. The civil society organizations themselves are not democratically legitimized: there is no guarantee that they will represent the interests of a majority of citizens; they are in some cases representatives of specific interests; and their concerns are often limited to a particular area of policy.

Even if civil society plays an important role in the political process, the final binding decision on sovereign measures must still be left to democratically legitimized institutions. The latter not only have the task of weighing different points of view, arguments, and contributions against each other and taking them into account in the decision-making process; importantly, they also have to work towards ensuring that the participation of civil society expresses the broadest possible spectrum of different views in society and that individual interests do not exert undue influence.

Notes

1. German Federal Agency for Civic Education, "NGOs
   – Nicht-Regierungsorganisationen," October 1, 2017,
   https://www.bpb.de/nachschlagen/zahlen-und-fakten/
   globalisierung/52808/ngos (accessed December 12, 2020).

2. Colin Crouch, "Neue Formen der Partizipation" in
   Forschungsjournal Soziale Bewegung, 29 (3) (2016), p. 143 ff.

3. The German Bundestag is looking into this issue and in
   the late 1990s set up a commission of inquiry, "The Future
   of Civic Engagement," which aims to develop concrete
   political strategies and measures to promote voluntary,
   public welfare-oriented, non-materialistic civic engagement
   in Germany. On June 3, 2002 this commission presented
   its extensive report: Bundestag document 14/8900 v.
   3.6.2002; The growing influence of civil society led to the
   establishment of the project "Civil Society in Numbers"
   (ZiviZ), which is supported by the Bertelsmann Foundation,
   the Stifterverband für die Deutsche Wissenschaft [Donors'
   Association for the Promotion of Humanities and Sciences in
   Germany], and the Fritz Thyssen Foundation. ZiviZ aims, in
   particular, to improve the data pool relating to civil society,
   providing analysis, advice, and networking as a "think &
   do tank," and giving new impetus to the establishment of a
   strong civil society: cf. Zivilgesellschaft in Zahlen,
   https://www.ziviz.info (accessed December 12, 2020).

4. For a very instructive discussion of the various attempts
   at definition with numerous references, see: Saskia
   Richter, "Zivilgesellschaft – Überlegungen zu einem
   interdisziplinären Konzept" version: 1.0 in *Docupedia-
   Zeitgeschichte,* March 8, 2016, http://docupedia.de/zg/
   richter_zivilgesellschaft_v1_de_2016 (accessed December
   12, 2020); cf. also the description in the Opinion of the
   Economic and Social Committee on the subject: "Die Rolle

und der Beitrag der organisierten Zivilgesellschaft zum europäischen Einigungswerk," September 22, 1999 (1999/C 329/10), Official Journal no. C 329, November 17, 1999, p. 30.

5. Rupert Graf Strachwitz, *Basiswissen Zivilgesellschaft*, (Opuscula 140) (Berlin: Maecenata Institut für Philanthropie und Zivilgesellschaft, July 2020), https://nbn-resolving. org/urn:nbn:de:0168-ssoar-68884-0 (accessed December 12, 2020); the following remarks are also taken from this publication.

6. For example, the Nobel Peace Prize was awarded in 2017 to the International Campaign to Abolish Nuclear Weapons, in 2013 to the Organization for the Prohibition of Chemical Weapons, in 1999 to Doctors without Borders, and in 1997 to the International Campaign to Ban Landmines.

7. An extensive discussion with numerous references can be found in: Barbara Unmüßig, "Zivilgesellschaft unter Druck – shrinking – closing – nospace," Heinrich Böll Foundation, May 2016, https://www.boell.de/sites/default/files/uploads/2016/03/zivilgesellschaft_unter_druck_shrinking_spaces.pdf (accessed December 12, 2020).

8. German political foundations were also among those affected, such as the Konrad Adenauer Foundation, the Friedrich Ebert Foundation, the Heinrich Böll Foundation, and the Friedrich Naumann Foundation.

9. Cf. Tatjana Gluschkova, "Neuer Gesetzesentwurf engt Spielraum von NGOs weiter ein," Memorial Deutschland, November 2020, https://www.memorial.de/index.php/7872-neuer-gesetzentwurf-engt-spielraum-von-ngos-weiter-ein (accessed December 12, 2020).

10. See: Amnesty International, "Ägypten: neues repressives NGO-Gesetz verabschiedet," July 15, 2019, https://www.amnesty.ch/de/laender/naher-osten-nordafrika/aegypten/dok/2019/neues-repressives-ngo-gesetz-verabschiedet# (accessed December 12, 2020); the Konrad Adenauer Stiftung was forced by the Egyptian government to leave

the country: cf. Robert Roßmann, "Das Problem mit den Punkten auf der Weltkarte," *Süddeutsche Zeitung*, November 11, 2020, https://www.sueddeutsche.de/politik/konrad-adenauer-stiftung-norbert-lammert-1.5125266 (accessed December 12, 2020).

11. Judgment of the Court of Justice of the European Union, June 18, 2020, Case C 78/18, EuZW 2020, 858.

12. On this subject, see also: Tanja Brühl, "Mehr Raum für die unbequemen Mitspieler?" in Achim Brunnengräber, Ansgar Klein and Heike Walk (eds.), *NGOs als Legitimationsressource: Zivilgesellschaftliche Partizipationsformen im Globalisierungsprozess* (Berlin: Springer, 2013), p. 137 ff.

13. Cf. Opinion of the Economic and Social Committee.

14. Regulation (EU) 2019/788 of the European Parliament and Council of April 17, 2019, on the European Citizens' Initiative.

15. Cf. "Allianz Vielfältige Demokratie und Bertelsmannstiftung, Partizipative Gesetzgebung – Ein Modell zur Beteiligung von Bürgerinnen und Bürgern an Gesetzgebungsverfahren," (2017), https://www.bertelsmann-stiftung.de/en/ publications/publication/did/partizipative-gesetzgebung (accessed December 12, 2020).

16. "Wissenschaftliche Dienste des Deutschen Bundestages, Neue Formen demokratischer Beteiligung von Bürgern," Draft paper v. 21.2.2018, WD3-3000-03718, https://www.bundestag.de/resource/ blob/550340/1cfa9b21f88835679b09f0eec7bf60c0/WD-3-037-18-pdf-data.pdf (accessed December 12, 2020).

17. Cf. Heike Walk, Achim Brunnengräber, and Ansgar Klein, "NGOs – die 'Entschleuniger' der Globalisierung?" in Achim Brunnengräber, Ansgar Klein, and Heike Walk (eds.), *NGOs als Legitimationsressource: Zivilgesellschaftliche Partizipationsformen im Globalisierungsprozess* (Berlin: Springer, 2013), p. 14.

18. Wolf-Dieter Narr, "INGOs, Himalaya-Gebirge, Ozeane und raumenthobene Demokratie" in Achim Brunnengräber, Ansgar Klein, and Heike Walk (eds.), *NGOs als Legitimationsressource: Zivilgesellschaftliche Partizipationsformen im Globalisierungsprozess* (Berlin: Springer, 2013), p. 53.

19. On the difficulty of engaging with political legitimacy, see: Luisa Girnus, *Politische Legitimation und politisches Lernen* (Berlin: Springer, 2019), p. 11.

20. Cf. among others, Ulf Kemper, *Politische Legitimität und politischer Raum im Wandel* (Berlin: Springer, 2015).

21. On the different concepts see for example, Joachim Blatter, "Demokratie und Legitimation" in Arthur Benz, Susanne Lütz, Uwe Schimank, and Georg Simonis (eds.), *Handbuch Governance* (Berlin: Springer, 2007).

22. Specifically, Ernst-Wolfgang Böckenförde, "Demokratie als Verfassungsprinzip" in Josef Isensee and Paul Kirchhof (eds.), *Handbuch des Staatsrechts*, 3rd edn. (2004), § 24 note 14 ff.

23. In particular, Torsten Stein, "Demokratische Legitimierung auf supranationaler und internationaler Ebene" in *Heidelberg Journal of International Law*, (64) 2004, p. 563.

24. Cf. reporting only: Armin von Bogdandy, "Demokratie, Globalisierung, Zukunft des Völkerrechts – eine Bestandsaufnahme" in *Heidelberg Journal of International Law*, (63) (2003), p. 853 (873).

25. Peter-Tobias Stoll, *Globalisierung und Legitimation*, quoted in von Bogdandy, "Demokratie, Globalisierung," note 81.

26. Stein, "Demokratische Legitimierung," p. 563.

27. von Bogdandy, "Demokratie, Globalisierung," p. 853 (874).

CHAPTER 5

THE "SOCIAL RESPONSIBILITY" OF BUSINESS: NEW ALLIANCES BETWEEN POLITICS AND THE ECONOMY?

CLEMENS FUEST

In debates about economic and social ills, businesses are repeatedly criticized for maximizing their profits while neglecting their social and public responsibility. Such criticism is not new, but against the backdrop of increasing inequality of income and wealth in many industrialized countries and growing concerns about the destruction of the environment and a lack of sustainability, it is acquiring new urgency. The demand that businesses give up their focus on profit maximization contrasts sharply with the conclusions of economic theory, according to which profit maximization in a competitive economy can also, under certain conditions, improve overall economic welfare.

This essay examines the demand for businesses to focus on the goals of society overall, and it comes to three main conclusions. First, profit maximization in businesses also serves the common good, provided certain conditions are met. These conditions include rules ensuring that costs are allocated correctly and preventing businesses from abusing their market power at the expense of their customers or their employees and suppliers. Second, we should not expect too much from the practice—frequently demanded and widely used—of embedding goals relating to the common good in corporate governance. It is not the job of managers to use the corporate resources that do not belong to them to pursue goals that are not those of their employers. Political regulations for business that encroach on owners' rights are allowed because they have been democratically legitimized. By contrast, the actions of managers are not and cannot replace political intervention. Third, maximizing profits can also take the form of corporate stakeholders influencing the political process at the expense of the common good. To curb this, it is of the utmost importance that political decision-making processes are transparent, including the work of lobby groups and the role of donations in funding political parties. Alliances between politics and the economy should therefore lie primarily in joint support for these rules, rather than in a symbiotic cooperation, which can easily lead to collusion at the expense of third parties. A certain distance and a clear division and delimitation of responsibility between decision-makers in business and politics are necessary.

The argument continues as follows. The analysis begins with Milton Friedman's "classic" and provocative doctrine, which says that the social responsibility of business lies precisely in maximizing their profits. The second section discusses the relationship between individual interests and the overall social welfare. Section three explains the conditions under which profit maximization by companies serves the common good. The fourth section deals with policy failures in the form of companies influencing government frameworks to their own benefit. Section five examines the consequences for the common good if companies fail to maximize their profits because managers pursue goals other than those of the owners. The sixth section discusses the idea of increasingly incorporating goals pertaining to the common good into corporate governance. The seventh section presents my conclusions.

1. THE FRIEDMAN DOCTRINE ON THE SOCIAL RESPONSIBILITY OF BUSINESS

"The social responsibility of business is to increase its profits." This is the provocative title of an essay by Nobel Prize-winning economist Milton Friedman which appeared in the *New York Times* on September 13, 1970.[1] It is considered one of the most influential newspaper articles of the past few decades, but it has also attracted an unusually high level of criticism. The article was prompted by demands at the time for businesses not to maximize profits, but pursue other goals such as charity for the benefit of the "poor," environmental protection, education, or generally the welfare of society as a whole. Even today, such demands are made time and again, combined with the accusation that a focus on profit maximization is morally reprehensible and harmful from a macroeconomic perspective.

Milton Friedman rejects the premise that businesses should be committed to goals that deviate from the interests of their owners as totalitarian and incompatible with a free society. He points out that the demand to demonstrate "social responsibility" is made primarily of managers of large companies, typically listed corporations, rather than of sole traders who are both managers and owners of their company. Friedman argues that listed corporation managers are employed by the owners alone. If business owners decide to pursue goals other than profit maximization, that is fine, because they can dispose of their own property. If managers who do not own the business do this, they are doing things with other people's money that they were not employed to do. If the owners cannot prevent the managers from doing so, it is as if the managers are taxing the owners and using the tax money as they see fit. They are thus acting like a government agency that raises taxes and decides how the income is used.

In a liberal democracy, the task of raising taxes and deciding how to use the money rests with parliaments and the governments appointed by them. The point at which the state's claims to taxation end is the point where the private sector begins, where people can freely decide—within the framework of the law—how to use their property and resources. Engaging managers of private businesses for state goals ultimately means submitting the private sector to political decision-making processes. According to Milton Friedman, this is nothing more than the replacement of the market economy with a socialist economic order in which political processes determine the use of resources.

In the public debate about how businesses conduct themselves and what goals they should set themselves, Milton Friedman's doctrine is often viewed as an extreme position and criticized accordingly.[2] At the same time, his article is regarded as an intellectual basis for the so-called "shareholder value" approach, according to which managers should increase the market value of their company's shares. This is nothing other than profit maximization applied to the case of listed corporations.

2. INDIVIDUAL INTERESTS AND THE WELFARE OF SOCIETY

Can a society, whose members primarily aim to serve their own individual interests, function and create prosperity for broad strata of society? Analyzing this question, which relates mainly to market-based systems, has been the focus of economic research for many years and is hotly debated in related social-science disciplines too. This research must first clarify whether the pursuit of one's own interests is to be regarded as a fundamental constant in human behavior, taking the term "self-interest" in a broad sense. Most people are not narrowly egotistical. On the contrary, the willingness to cooperate and a sense of empathy are important human characteristics.[3] Nevertheless, there is good empirical evidence that their personal advantage and that of their family and friends are usually more important to them than the interests of the general population of the country in which they live, or even of the global population. If answer to this is yes, this means that societies always consist of members who pursue their individual interests, regardless of whether it is a market economy, a centrally planned economy, or some other system. From this perspective, the success of a society depends on whether its institutions channel and coordinate the behavior of its members in such a way that individual people also serve the common good by pursuing their own interests.

It is one of the great advantages of a market economy that it can manage to do this. Adam Smith's notion of the "invisible hand" says that by pursuing their personal goals and interests in a market economy, people are serving the common good at the same time in unintended ways. Entrepreneurs who are in competition with one another and competing for customers benefit when they offer the goods that consumers want at the lowest possible cost. Competition forces them to do so at prices that are not too far removed from cost price. In a centrally planned economy, people also pursue their individual interests, but history tells us that this leads to poverty, restrictions on freedom, and damage to the environment. There is a lack of incentives to use resources sparingly and to consider the wishes of others—for example the customers of a business. There is also a lack of the kind of information-processing that the pricing system provides. So it's not about whether people are pursuing their own interests—they always do. It depends on the framework in which this happens.

In modern economics, the so-called first theorem of welfare economics can be seen as a manifestation of the idea of the "invisible hand": every competitive equilibrium is Pareto optimal. In a society in which goods are traded in markets that have flexible prices and competition, companies pursue profit maximization as their exclusive goal and consumers also pursue just their individual interests, market interaction creates macroeconomic efficiency; that means that changes in market outcomes cannot put anyone in a better position without someone becoming worse off.

Two aspects of this finding are important, however. First, it says nothing about distributional issues. It's all about the size of the "cake," not how it's divided. Second, it is based on premises that are often violated under real economic circumstances. Market power, asymmetric distribution of information, externalities, rigid prices and liquidity constraints, and incomplete contracts are all reasons why market outcomes are often inefficient. However, it does not necessarily follow that state intervention leads to improvements.

As for the question of whether businesses that maximize their profits serve the common good, it should be added that in a world that upholds the premises on which the first theorem of welfare economics is based, there would be no businesses with permanent employees, and certainly not the large corporations with thousands of employees that we know today. In a frictionless economy, all services would be traded on markets. Long-term employment contracts and administrative structures would be superfluous. The fact that companies are complex organizations with multiple principal–agent relationships has implications for this debate.

3. DO BUSINESSES THAT MAXIMIZE THEIR PROFITS SERVE THE COMMON GOOD? THE PROBLEM OF MARKET FAILURE

The doctrine that companies can best serve the common good by maximizing their profits is a powerful one, provided that the above requirements of the first theorem of welfare economics are met. But that is not always the case. For example, if companies cause environmental damage without being asked to pay for it appropriately, or if they consult with their competitors and create cartels, then maximizing profits does not lead to the maximization of economic welfare overall. In economic theory such cases are known as market failure.

However, it does not necessarily follow that companies should pursue goals other than maximizing their profits. It's primarily the task of politics to respond to this market failure. Environmental taxes or regulations should ensure that the costs of economic activity, as they affect the macroeconomy, also appear in a business's private accounts. The task of competition policy is to prevent cartels and other restrictions on competition. Companies that have market power for technological reasons, for example telecommunications operators or energy networks, are regulated so that they do not abuse their market power to the detriment of consumers. In terms of information, pharmaceutical businesses have significant advantages over patients, and often over the doctors who are prescribing their drugs. Approval processes and regulations should ensure that drugs are prescribed safely and appropriately.

The macroeconomic and social effects of social media are also increasingly coming in for criticism. Companies such as Facebook and TikTok maximize their profits by competing for users' attention. The more time users spend on these media, the higher the advertising revenue. In this kind of competition, users are systematically sent messages that match their observed preferences or inclinations so that they stay on the respective platform for as long as possible. This has various consequences. On the one hand, this results in a tendency towards polarization, the dissemination of fake news, or the targeted manipulation of political opinions and even elections.[4] On the other hand, addictive behaviors can arise with highly negative consequences for the health of those affected.[5] The abuse of communication tools and addiction risks exist with regard to many other products. In these cases, state regulation should guarantee the right balance between consumer sovereignty and consumer protection, including the protection of children and young people.

So if the state provides the right framework, market disruptions can be resolved. If there is a public demand for businesses to refrain from maximizing profits and voluntarily pursue other goals, for example environmental protection goals or other interests for the common good, economists usually reject this, demanding instead that the state set an appropriate framework. If that happens, we do not have to rely on businesses responding to appeals and changing their behavior accordingly. If it is true that people primarily pursue their own interests, then we cannot assume that such appeals will have much impact—in order to achieve something, we have to change the legal framework. However, economists also like to emphasize that there are not only market failures, but also government failures. Therefore, referring the problem to a state-provided framework is only partially satisfactory. Equally, the risk that government intervention might be unavailable or might fail has in part to do with corporate behavior.

4. STATE-PROVIDED FRAMEWORK AND THE INFLUENCE OF BUSINESS: ONE VERSION OF POLITICAL FAILURE

Appropriate interventions in economic policy can correct many of the inefficiencies and malfunctions that arise due to the market imperfections we have described. However, frictions exist not only in private markets; in the political process too, there are extensive problems concerning information and incentive. Governments are not "omniscient, benevolent dictators," but institutions in which people, as in private markets, pursue their individual goals and in which different interests collide. Even if government action could remedy market disruptions in principle, political decision-making processes are by no means always the way of making this happen.

In political decision-making processes, interest groups have the opportunity of influencing laws and the actions of governments through the work of lobbyists. In many cases, legislation is almost impossible without representatives of the businesses or industries concerned providing information. This opens up a wide range of opportunities for influencing decisions. In many countries political parties are dependent on donations: this enables businesses and other financially powerful donors to make their wishes known to political decision-makers in a more or less subtle way.

When businesses maximize their profits by changing the economic rules in their favor, the result can be very damaging from a macroeconomic perspective. A much-discussed example is the regulation of banks and their contribution to the global financial crisis that erupted in 2008. For a long time, banks and their representatives have exerted influence over the political process of finance regulation leading to a great deal of leeway to operate with very little equity capital, to use complex calculation models for risk assessment that are difficult to understand by both the supervisory authorities and their own supervisory bodies, and to transform maturities on an extremely large scale.[6]

By doing so, many banks took enormous risks. As long as the economy was performing well, banks and especially bank managers generated extraordinarily high incomes and profits. That this was possible was due not only to lax banking regulation. Doing such business with very little equity would, under normal circumstances, have resulted in the banks' creditors demanding more equity or such high risk premiums that the business was not worthwhile. This did not happen, however, because the creditors could expect that banks in trouble would be bailed out by government support, because bank failures have widespread negative effects on the rest of the economy. When, to everyone's surprise, the investment bank Lehman Brothers was not bailed out with taxpayers' money in September 2008, massive disruptions occurred in the financial system. There was a collapse of confidence within the financial sector, which left other banks in trouble. These banks were then rescued through a massive injection of taxpayers' money.

In financial crises, therefore, governments are practically forced to bail out banks using taxpayers' money in order to prevent a serious economic crisis. As a result, profits that are made in good times go to the owners and managers of banks, while losses that happen during crises have to be borne by taxpayers. Profits are privatized, losses are socialized. From a macroeconomic perspective, this form of profit maximization, which is based on the implementation of distorted rules, has highly negative consequences. On the one hand, and very unfairly, a few get rich at the expense of the general public. On the other, banks are incentivized to enter into excessively risky transactions, creating a huge mismanagement of resources.

Lobbying is similarly influential in other highly regulated sectors, for example the pharmaceutical sector or in grid-based industries in energy supply or communications. The digital economy is also much interested in influencing the regulatory framework in its favor. In new research, Thomas Philippon describes how systematic lobbying by businesses and industry representatives in the United States has resulted in ever more restricted competition.[7] This has resulted in goods becoming increasingly expensive, corporate profits growing, wages of employees falling, and consumers becoming disadvantaged because they have to pay excessive prices or receive poor-quality products.

Lobbying is part and parcel of the democratic process and is protected by a set of fundamental rights. Equally, it can certainly be productive for the overall society if lobbying means that information is introduced into the political process resulting in better laws. However, lobbying often leads to particular interests being privileged at the expense of the common good.

In addition to legal lobbying, there are cases of corruption. There are times when businesses or individuals bribe government decision-makers and gain advantages, often at the expense of the local population. For example, this can take the form of environmental laws not being complied with and not monitored by the state, or overpriced public contracts being awarded at the expense of domestic taxpayers. This kind of influence over government activities is the subject of intensive debate in developing and emerging countries, where governance structures are poorly developed and media checks do not work well. However, corruption exists in highly developed democracies based on the rule of law as well.

It is obvious that profit maximization in the form of lobbying for state-granted privileges or even corruption can cause a great deal of damage to the society. It has thus been shown that businesses focusing on the goal of profit maximization is more compatible with the goal of maximizing the overall societal welfare, the more government action is geared towards this goal. However, if government action does not respond appropriately to cases of market failure or if particular interests are placed above the common good when political decisions are made, private profit maximization can cause considerable damage to society as a whole.

5. WHAT ARE THE CONSEQUENCES FOR THE COMMON GOOD IF BUSINESS DOES NOT MAXIMIZE ITS PROFITS AT ALL?

In reality, businesses are not atomistic units that mechanically maximize profits, but complex and sometimes extremely large organizations that are run by an administrative apparatus. Since the senior managers are usually not the owners, it is *a priori* unclear whether they have an interest in maximizing the business's profits.

The managers' remuneration is often linked to the share price. Share prices are probably the best available indicator for determining the business's value, corresponding to the current value of future profits. Aligning the managers' interests with the interests of the owners is nevertheless a complex task that does not go smoothly. If managers use monies from the business for projects that are more useful to them personally than to the business, this can have negative consequences not only for the owners, but also for the overall economy. For example, managers such as Ford's Jacques Nasser, Jack Smith at General Motors, and Juergen Schrempp at Daimler have been accused of "empire-building" and being responsible for serious misinvestments.[8] These bad investments are not only painful for the owners, they are also harmful to the overall economy. In these cases, the cause of the damage is not too much but rather too little profit maximization.

The issue of the decision-makers' horizons plays an important role in the current debate about the role of sustainability in the private sector. Managers are often accused of taking excessively high salaries and focusing too much on short-term successes, such as quarterly results. Profit maximization in the interests of the owners basically means long-term, sustainable maximization of profits. The issue of long-term, but slowly progressing changes is a controversial topic. One example is climate change and political measures to contain it and adapt to rising temperatures. This raises the question of whether the governance structures of businesses ensure that the consequences of this development for their own business model are appropriately included in management decisions. If many businesses do not take this on board, it can also become more difficult for politicians to implement the necessary adjustments. For example, it is more problematic to increase the price of CO_2 if companies have not invested in climate-friendly technologies. In this context, Mark Carney describes the "tragedy of the horizon"—a reference to the "tragedy of the commons."[9] It is important that managers' contracts and corporate governance avoid creating incentives for short-term profit maximization at the expense of medium- and long-term development.

Maximizing shareholder value means that in functioning capital markets share prices do not depend primarily on quarterly earnings, but on the expected long-term development of a business. There is, however, friction in capital markets, due among other things to the fact that managers are usually better informed about their business than external investors. This is why long-term orientation simply by maximizing the market value has its limits. However, it is not easy to find better indicators for the sustainability of earnings than capital market valuations.

6. SHOULD WE INCLUDE THE GOALS OF SOCIETY IN CORPORATE GOVERNANCE?

Time and again demands are made to anchor the goals of the overall society within corporate governance and to oblige managers to align their activities with these goals and not just with the wishes of the owners. This is already the case in many businesses, although it is not always clear how binding and relevant the published goals might be. This is problematic for a number of reasons. As Milton Friedman explained, this way of linking private property to politically set goals seems like an encroachment on property rights. This is not problematic *per se*—lots of laws such as tax laws, environmental regulations, and building regulations have the same effect. It becomes problematic when the managers employed by the owners are given too much discretion in defining social concerns such as sustainability and incorporating them into business decisions. In particular, such clauses can exacerbate the principal–agent problem between owners and managers. Managers may, for example, have an interest in using the money belonging to the company owners to make a name for themselves by promoting ecological or social causes; this is not legitimate, however. The use of taxpayers' money is legitimate because and to the extent that it is subject to democratic control. Managers are not controlled in this way, but rather by the business owners.

7. CONCLUSION: EFFECTIVENESS AND TRANSPARENCY IN GOVERNMENT ACTIVITIES ARE CRUCIAL

In order to prevent the activities of businesses from running counter to legitimate concerns of the society, the state-provided framework is crucial. The more precisely the external effects of entrepreneurial activity are internalized, the more effectively market power is contained and competition protected, the more compatible are the owners' interests in high profits and the interests of the overall economy.

From this perspective, the division of labor between businesses and governments lies in the fact that the latter should ensure, through an appropriate framework, that private profit-seeking is equally productive for the overall economy. However, it should not be overlooked that the political process itself is influenced by business and their lobby groups. Profit maximization can also mean changing the framework for one's own benefit, in some cases at the expense of the common good. For a market-based economy to succeed, therefore, it is crucial to ensure that government actions focusing on the common good are maintained through the transparency of political decision-making processes, including the cooperation of political decision-makers with lobby groups and donors, particularly in the financing of political parties.

These goals will not be served if businesses replace profit orientation with a focus on the common good, thereby blurring the boundaries between government tasks and corporate responsibility. On the contrary, a certain distance between politics and businesses is necessary to avoid conflicts of interest and giving the impression that businesses and political decision-makers are in collusion. From the societal point of view, productive alliances between politics and business should not primarily mean interdependencies and close cooperation between representatives of business and political decision-makers, but rather a shared awareness of the rules that must be adhered to so that the individual profit-seeking really serves the common good.

Notes

1. Milton Friedman, "The Social Responsibility of Business is to Enhance its Profits" in *New York Times Magazine* 32 (13) (1970), pp. 122–26.

2. For an up-to-date critique of the Friedman doctrine, see for example Martin Wolf, "Milton Friedman was Wrong on the Corporation: The Doctrine that has Guided Economists and Businesses for 50 Years needs Re-evaluation" in *The Financial Times*, December 8, 2020, https://www.ft.com/content/e969a756-922e-497b-8550-94bfb1302cdd (accessed February 9, 2021).

3. This is the point made by Collier and Kay, for example. Paul Collier and John Kay, *Greed is Dead—Politics after Individualism* (London: Penguin Random House, 2020).

4. See Carl T. Bergstrom and Joseph B. Bak-Coleman (2019), "Gerrymandering in Social Networks" in *Nature* 573, (2019), pp. 40–41; Gillian Murphy, Elizabeth F. Loftus, Rebecca Hofstein Grady, Linda J. Levine, and Ciara M. Greene, "False Memories for Fake News during Ireland's Abortion Referendum" in *Psychological Science* 30, (2019), pp. 1449–59.

5. Cf. Qinghua He, Ofir Turel, and Antoine Bechara, "Brain Anatomy Alterations associated with Social Networking Site (SNS) Addiction" in *Scientific Reports* 7, 45064 (2017).

6. For example, see Anat Admati and Martin Hellwig, *The Bankers' New Clothes* (Princeton: Princeton University Press, 2013), in particular Chapter 12 (pp. 192 f), which explains why banks have been successful lobbyists over many years and to some extent continue to be.

7. Thomas Philippon, *The Great Reversal: How America Gave up on Free Markets* (Cambridge MA: The Belknap Press, 2019).

8. https://www.autonews.com/article/20090505/ BLOG01/905059984/watch-out-here-comes-another-empire-builder (accessed February 9, 2021).

9. Mark Carney, "Breaking the Tragedy of the Horizon— Climate Change and Financial Stability." Speech by Mark Carney, Governor of the Bank of England and Chairman of the Financial Stability Board, at Lloyd's of London, London, September 29, 2015, https://www.bankofengland.co.uk/ speech/2015/breaking-the-tragedy-of-the-horizon-climate-change-and-financial-stability (accessed December 9, 2020).

CHAPTER 6

ARE INTERNATIONAL ORGANIZATIONS THE TRAGIC HEROES OF WORLD POLITICS?

EUGÉNIA C. HELDT

INTRODUCTION

Are international organizations (IOs) the tragic heroes of world politics today? If they are too successful and accomplish their tasks in full, they risk being abolished. If they assert their independence and autonomy by going beyond their delegation mandates, they are criticized by government leaders and by the media. Why are IOs increasingly being pilloried? Why are they under continuous pressure, stress, and somehow in a kind of permanent crisis? And how did we get there?

In order to understand the current challenging situation, it is useful to remember how it all began. IOs have existed for over 200 years and since then not only has their number steadily increased, but so too has the scope and complexity of their responsibilities and duties. In the early 20th century there were around 30 international institutions; today there are over 7,700. The majority of the international institutions and organizations that exist today, such as the United Nations, were founded in the postwar period. The subtle retreat and disengagement of the hegemon, the United States, China's rise as a new potential world power, but also the fragmentation of the institutional landscape and the associated emergence of new informal forms of governance – including the G7, G8, and G20 summits – pose enormous challenges for transnational cooperation and demonstrate how multilateralism is under attack from many different directions. A few examples from current challenges in global governance illustrate this:

- In the case of the World Trade Organization (WTO), the United States is blocking the re-appointment of judges to the Appellate Body, thus torpedoing the WTO's functionality.

- In the midst of the COVID-19 pandemic, the United States and Brazil announced that they intended to withdraw from the World Health Organization (WHO).

- The Brexit referendum and the UK's subsequent exit from the EU represent a turning point in the European integration process. The completion of Brexit in 2020 has put paid to any illusions about the irreversibility of the European integration process.

- The European Central Bank (ECB) may well have saved the Euro, but since the Euro crisis it has been faced with accusations such as breach of contract and exceeding its mandate. The latest ruling by the German Federal Constitutional Court on the purchase of bonds represents another high point in this controversy.

All these events show that today IOs are more controversial than ever. Some states are now even considering giving up their membership in these multilateral forums. It was no coincidence that the UKIP party's Brexit campaign motto was "Vote Leave, Take Control" or that Donald Trump ran an "America First" campaign during the US presidential election campaign.

In order to understand why IOs are currently in permanent crisis mode and their authority is increasingly being contested, in this essay I will look at the main topics and waves of research in the area of International Relations and offer explanations as to why multilateralism in general and international institutions and organizations in particular are being challenged. In so doing, I will examine the following three areas that have shaped research on IOs over the past decades: (1) the creation, delegation of competences, and empowerment of IOs; (2) the politicization of and challenges to their authority; and (3) the adaptability and resilience of IOs. My essay concludes with an appeal for more multilateralism.

1. THE CREATION, DELEGATION OF COMPETENCES, AND EMPOWERMENT OF IOS

When states decide to set up IOs instead of acting bilaterally, the following questions arise: why are

IOs created, which tasks do they perform, and which competences are delegated to them?

Before answering these questions, it is important to know what constitutes IOs. In International Relations, a discipline in the political sciences, a distinction is made between four types of international institution: organizations, regimes, networks, and sets of norms. International institutions are permanent and interconnected systems of rules and norms (both formal and informal) that prescribe instructions on how to behave, restrict activities, and determine expectations of behavior.[1] IOs, by contrast, are founded on the basis of an international treaty; include more than three Member States; have a permanent administrative structure, for example, a secretariat; exercise decision-making powers (both delegated and self-determined); and can therefore operate as or be considered to be actors.[2]

This brings us to the next point, which is the tasks to be assumed by IOs. They act as mediators between states; they serve as a collection point for information; they define expectations of appropriate state behavior; provide monitoring mechanisms; identify breaches of norms and rules; legitimize and/or impose sanctions; regulate the access of non-state actors to international negotiations; implement various programs and projects in numerous countries around the world. But how did it all start? Why do states at a certain point decide to promote international cooperation in the form of multilateral organizations and institutions instead of acting unilaterally?

Lessons from the Great Depression of the 1930s, the rise of fascist aggressor states, and the horrors of World War II led to the determination of statesmen such as Winston Churchill and Franklin D. Roosevelt to create new international structures to deal with problems that were inherently transnational. This resolve to learn from the mistakes of the past led to the creation of structures that would enable better multilateral cooperation in the future. Multilateralism founded on a rules-based world order with strong IOs were to ensure peace and prosperity, while reducing poverty and unemployment and promoting free trade and human rights worldwide. As a result, the United Nations and the Bretton Woods institutions (the World Bank and the International Monetary Fund [IMF]) were established. The Rome Treaties, signed in 1957, brought into being the supranational institutions and set in motion the European integration process. With the founding of the European Economic Community (EEC), the six Member States decided to transfer their sovereignty in certain policy areas to the EEC. Integration thus means the voluntary surrender of competences to the supranational entity of the EU. The EU experiment is now being copied in other regions of the world, in the shape of such organizations as Mercosur or ASEAN, for example.

Although international and European institutions have become a central part of the world order over time, they are highly controversial. In fulfilling their tasks, they intervene in states' sovereignty and independently adopt new competences. This in turn leads to disputes with the member states or to a great deal of public criticism. Sometimes IOs are accused of having got out of control and behaving like agents running amok.[3]

I have described international organizations as the tragic heroes of international politics, because if they work too closely with the Member States, they are seen as puppets controlled by the most powerful states in the system—as the current criticism of the WHO's close cooperation with China demonstrates. If, on the other hand, they emancipate themselves and act on their own initiative—as shown in the creative role taken by the ECB during the Euro crisis[4]—they are accused of abuse of power.

In the project "Delegation of Power and Empowerment of International Organizations over Time" (financed by the European Research Council) for the first time we systematically collected data on the competences and material resources (budget and staffing) of six of the most important IOs from their creation to today. In addition, we quantified and examined the empowerment process—defined as the transfer of competences and material resources—of IOs.[5] One of the main findings of this project was that IOs can strategically use financial and human resources for their own benefit, i.e. for their own empowerment.[6] On the basis of the principal–agent approach, we examined which tasks had been delegated to IOs and what resources member states have made available to them from their establishment in the early 1950s until today. Using the example of the EU, we are able to illustrate this empowerment process very well over time. Ever since the EU Member States decided in the 1960s to give the European Commission exclusive competence in trade policy in order to negotiate appropriate agreements with other countries from a position of strength (as a single entity), the Commission has represented the EU Member States at WTO negotiations.

Our studies in this project show that the gradual process of empowerment of these new actors went hand-in-hand with an expansion of oversight mechanisms, since in some cases states considered that IOs and European institutions had exceeded the competences delegated to them and acted against the interests of their member states—in principal–agent language, this is known as "agency slack." Thus, global institutions have sometimes been portrayed as "errant agents"[7] and as institutional "Frankensteins"[8] who have liberated themselves from the control of their principals (member states). In this research on IOs, therefore, the central question arises: under what conditions within IOs does "agency slack" occur, i.e. deviation from the mandate and behavior contrary to the intention of the principals?

The majority of studies in this area so far overlook the fact that "agency slack" can also be a positive side-effect of the transfer of power. IOs have been given a margin of discretion and autonomy so that they can operate as independent actors and carry out not just the tasks member states expect of them. In another research project at the Chair of European and Global Governance at the Department of Governance at the Technical University of Munich, we are comparing 25 UN organizations in order to conceptualize and operationalize "agency slack" for the first time and to show what necessary and sufficient conditions are required for it to occur. We have found that the organizational structure, particularly the IOs' margin of discretion when hiring staff, is a necessary condition for "agency slack" to emerge.

The "suspicion" of agency slack, that is, the unauthorized overstepping of their competences and the limitation of national sovereignty—be it in the Appellate Body of the WTO or the role of the ECB in the Euro crisis[9]—has over the last few years increasingly led to politicization and disputes about the legitimacy of the action taken by non-majoritarian institutions.

2. POLITICIZATION AND CHALLENGES TO AUTHORITY

In recent decades, the transfer of competences to IOs has led to a quantitative and qualitative increase in the importance of these institutions. Quantitative because there is hardly any policy area that is not regulated at least by some international institutions and organizations; and qualitative, because international norms and rules now have "legal status" in national legal systems.[10] The empowerment of IOs led to the juridification of international relations. This in turn contributed to questions of legitimacy and to a politicization of their actions. Some of the most frequent accusations are the abuse of power in the form of rape by UN Blue

Helmets in Bosnia; dysfunctional internal organizational structures; expensive international bureaucrats; the inability to reform the UN governance structure with its five veto powers (a relic of the postwar period); a lack of legitimacy; and few accountability mechanisms. Concerns about the legitimacy and accountability of IOs peaked in the 1990s in the context of the corruption scandals at the World Bank and the diminishing relevance of the IMF. This culminated in the "50 Years is Enough" campaign aimed at abolishing the World Bank and the IMF. This wave of politicization resulted in the World Bank reforming itself internally and developing new adaptation strategies in order to become more resilient. It increased cooperation with non-governmental organizations and established internal accountability mechanisms. Today the World Bank is one of the world's most transparent organizations.[11] This was also translated into the expansion of democratic influence over its activities, including improved access for civil society; increased transparency in the decision-making process; and accountability within the World Bank itself.[12]

In the meantime, the challenge lies not only in the lack of accountability, but also in what it means for the world order if democratic progress is undermined by power shifts in global governance. The rise of autocratically governed countries, such as China, limits the democratic influence on IOs and can thus in the long term lead to the decline of global democracy. Autocracies primarily want to expand their national sovereignty and give IOs as little involvement as possible. When they establish new IOs, they make sure that the mechanisms of democratic control are weak.[13]

3. ADAPTABILITY AND RESILIENCE

Another question is how IOs deal with the aforementioned kinds of criticism.[14] Previous responses from IOs included increasing transparency in decision-making processes, opening up to the outside world, developing new communications strategies, expanding their own mandate, or introducing more accountability mechanisms. Many of them have also ventured into new fields of activity as an adaptation strategy. The IMF and the World Bank have expanded their mandate to such an extent that critics accuse them of "getting bogged down." Today, the World Bank's interpretation of the term "development" encompasses environmental, pandemic, education, and even gender issues. Representatives of civil society, but also some member states, demanded that at least the IMF should concentrate on its core tasks, which include above all securing financial stability and promoting growth and trade, instead of dealing with issues such as economic inclusion, gender equality, inequality, poverty, and environmental protection in its analyses and funding programs.

Member states' dissatisfaction with the old IOs has contributed to the emergence of informal types of international cooperation such as the G7 and G20 formats—known as "minilateralism"[15]—that weaken multilateralism and more intensive institutionalized forms of cooperation. These alternative forums are more flexible and enable member states to react more quickly. The establishment of new, competing international and regional organizations has given rise to complex international regimes in which it is sometimes difficult to understand who the focal intergovernmental organization—i.e. the central point of contact—is in a particular policy area.

Today, the old international organizations have to cope with the shift in power that is taking place. For example, a study of "the decline of global democracy" demonstrates that the rise of countries such as China is undermining the democratic influence on IOs.[16] China's dissatisfaction with the old IOs, which are dominated by Western countries, has led to the establishment of alternative institutions such as the New Development Bank. This has enabled China to both circumvent the World Bank's good governance rules when allocating funds for development programs and strengthen its foothold in global politics. The emergence of new parallel structures has resulted in a fragmented institutional landscape. This represents another major challenge for the multilateral world order.

In the area of global Internet governance, for example, a variety of intergovernmental and non-governmental organizations exist. The retreat of states from this area has meant that a private company, the Internet Corporation for Assigned Names and Numbers (ICANN), is now responsible for assigning Internet addresses; by contrast the International Telecommunication Union (ITU) no longer plays a significant role. The same is true of the World Intellectual Property Organization (WIPO) and the WTO.

In the area of global health policy, the WHO is trying to regain its focus by increasing cooperation with member states during the COVID-19 pandemic through the so-called WHO Trial Initiative. The change in WHO funding from compulsory state contributions to voluntary contributions over the last few decades has now led to the organization being underfunded and global health policy being privatized. The WHO has had to seek out private donors and is now mostly funded by the Bill & Melinda Gates Foundation. This dependency on external/private donors has the unintended consequence that short-term results and successes have come to the fore and long-term disease control in the form of basic health programs has taken a back seat.

Another mystery in international relations is why IOs are almost never disbanded. Reforming or even abolishing existing IOs is a difficult undertaking, because in most cases all members have to agree. However, previous research in this area is often unsatisfactory and has mainly focused on individual organizations such as NATO.[17] For example, it is a mystery why NATO still exists today, even though the Cold War ended over 30 years ago.

CONCLUSION

Today more than ever we need a multilateral world order in which global interests take precedence over national interests. The current fragility of the multi-lateral system can only be overcome by strengthening multilateralism. This must be secured in legal terms so that IOs are not under constant attack from heads of state and government. At present, the International

Criminal Court, responsible for genocide and war crimes, is a toothless tiger, as the most powerful state in the system, the United States, does not recognize the Court and even calls it illegitimate. The WTO Appellate Body could face a similar fate. With its strong supranational institutions, such as the European Court of Justice, the EU could serve as a model for a stronger multilateral world order with strong IOs.

In order for IOs to emerge invigorated from the current crisis, we must also critically question whether the world really needs more than 7,000 international institutions or whether one central focal point for each policy area is sufficient. The IMF is a prime example of how a process of transformation can be successful. At the end of the 1990s, the IMF was on the verge of collapse because it ran out of "customers." During the financial crisis, the IMF with its specialist expertise rose again like a phoenix from the ashes. The same could happen to the WHO as a result of the COVID-19 pandemic. The current underfunding and consequent privatization of global health policy has meant that hardly any basic research in global health policy is going on, and that the WHO has not been able to respond adequately to the pandemic. We live in an interconnected world in which countries are dependent on each other—no country is a remote island. IOs are the central building blocks for maintaining and complying with the rules of the game of global governance. They need a margin of discretion in order to act independently of states and also to make uncomfortable but necessary decisions. Furthermore, they provide technical assistance in specific locations, act as mediators between states, help to overcome nationalism and territorial borders, make global governance more efficient, create a neutral framework using rules and procedures for the exchange of information, and serve as "arbitrators" in mediating interests and dealing with conflicts.

World peace is a fragile public good that can best be protected and strengthened through the cooperation and active contributions of international and European institutions. It would therefore be of central importance and an important signal if states would once again aspire to multilateral forms of cooperation and limit unilateral action, since "an institutionalized world is probably the worst form of governance—except for the alternatives."[18]

Notes

1. Robert O. Keohane, *International Institutions and State Power: Essays in International Relations Theory* (London and New York: Routledge, 1989), S. 3.

2. Eugénia da Conceição-Heldt, Martin Koch, and Andrea Liese (eds.), "Internationale Organisationen als Forschungsgegenstand. Oder: 'Über Blinde und die Gestalt des Elefanten'" in *Politische Vierteljahresschrift*, special issue 49 (2015), pp. 4–27, p. 9.

3. Eugénia da Conceição-Heldt, "Do Agents 'Run Amok'? Agency Slack in the EU and US Trade Policy in the Doha Round" in *Journal of Comparative Policy Analysis*, 15 (1) (2013), pp. 21–36.

4. Eugénia Heldt and Tony Mueller, "The (Self-)Empowerment of the European Central Bank during the Sovereign Debt Crisis" in *Journal of European Integration* (2020), pp. 1–16, DOI: 10.1080/07036337.2020.1729145.

5. For more information about the project see: https://delpowio.eu (accessed December 7, 2020).

6. Eugénia Heldt and Henning Schmidtke, "Measuring the Empowerment of International Organizations: The Evolution of Financial and Staff Capabilities" in *Global Policy* 8 (S5) 2017, pp. 51–61.

7. Eugénia Heldt, "Regaining Control of Errant Agents? Agency Slack at the European Commission and the World Health Organization" in *Cooperation and Conflict*, 52 (4) (2017), pp. 469–84.

8. Darren G. Hawkins, David A. Lake, Daniel L. Nielson, and Michael J. Tierney (eds.), *Delegation and Agency in International Organizations* (Cambridge: Cambridge University Press, 2006).

9. Heldt and Mueller, "The (Self-)Empowerment of the European Central Bank."

10. Conceição-Heldt, Koch, and Liese, "Internationale Organisationen als Forschungsgegenstand."

11. Eugénia Heldt, "Lost in Internal Evaluation? Accountability and Insulation at the World Bank" in *Contemporary Politics*, 24 (5) (2018), pp. 568–87.

12. Eugénia Heldt and Henning Schmidtke, "Global Democracy in Decline?" in *Global Governance: A Review of Multilateralism and International Organizations*, 25 (2) (2019), pp. 231–54.

13. Heldt and Schmidtke, "Global Democracy in Decline?".

14. Klaus Dingwerth, Antonia Witt, Ina Lehmann, Ellen Reichel and Tobias Weise (eds.), *International Organizations under Pressure: Legitimating Global Governance in Challenging Times* (Oxford: Oxford University Press, 2019).

15. K. Orfeo Fioretos, "Minilateralism and Informality in the International Monetary System" in *Review of International Political Economy*, 26 (6) (2019), pp. 1136–59.

16. Heldt and Schmidtke, "Global Democracy in Decline?"

17. Celeste A. Wallander, "Institutional Assets and Adaptability: NATO After the Cold War" in *International Organization*, 54 (4) (2003), pp. 705–35.

18. Robert O. Keohane, "Governance in a Partially Globalized World," Presidential Address, American Political Science Association, American Political Science Review, vol. 95, no 1, March 2001, https://spia.princeton.edu/system/files/research/documents/finalapsrpaper.pdf (accessed January 30, 2021).

CHAPTER 7

DO WE NEED A WORLD GOVERNMENT?

WOLFGANG SCHÖN

There is no world government. That's both wonderful and terrible. It's wonderful because it prevents total control of human life on our planet. It's wonderful because it gives anyone who disagrees with the political system in their country the right to seek a better life in another country. It's terrible because economic, cultural, and military conflicts between nations can escalate uncontrollably. It's terrible because a world government would be in a position to meet the global challenges facing humankind—from climate catastrophe via international migration to demographic change—in a purposeful way.

It's easy to agree that a world government is a sheer utopia, not just today but in the future as well. But two questions remain—one is theoretical, the other practical. The theoretical question addresses whether the positive aspects of global political rule would outweigh its negative consequences. And the practical question connected with this is whether states through their political activities should try to move ever closer to the goal of global governance.

Let's start with the first question: would world government be a good idea, all things considered? Of course this requires a differentiated approach. Would we conceive of the political system of such a world government as a dictatorship or a democracy? Nobody will want to live under a global dictatorship—that much seems clear at first glance. But we might object that in times of existential threat—just think of the climate catastrophe—perhaps only a tough command system would be able to enforce the massive sacrifices of personal freedom and economic prosperity that are required to avert the greatest possible damage to the environment and humanity. After all, in a period of great need the Romans handed the task of saving the *res publica* to a *dictator* for a limited time. However, the prerequisite for success would be not only a time limit on rulership, but also the personal suitability of the ruler. Experiences of contemporary dictators do not bode well. And even if autocrats or one-party regimes occasionally demonstrate an ability to act effectively, for example in the regulation and enforcement of compulsory measures to contain infectious diseases, we would not want to accept the collateral damage caused by a dictatorship, which ranges from rampant corruption to massive human rights violations. Finally, and by way of example, dictatorships do not have a good track record on environmental protection.

What would we think about a democratically legitimized world government? We are talking about the kind of state whose laws are enacted by a world parliament, whose institutions are controlled by a world justice system, and whose global policies would answer to a global electorate. Would that be a dream or a nightmare? First of all, the real economic, cultural, religious, and regional conflicts that shape the present day would not disappear immediately. They would only be transferred to become the internal concern of a unitary state—like all other political challenges. Any kind of foreign policy would become "global domestic policy" in the literal sense. And the success of the latter would be predicated on the assumption that both

the global and "domestic" dispute settlement mechanisms of such a world state can effectively deal with
these challenges. It's not easy: how is a democratically
organized world state with nearly eight billion citizens
supposed to cope with conflicts of interests between
highly diverse groups, between majorities and minorities on all continents? How is a world government
supposed to obtain the relevant information in
order to carry out its political tasks on the ground?
Which compulsory measures would be granted to a
world government that is supposed to have a global
monopoly on the use of force? How would we imagine
the financing of a world state whose inhabitants live
under dramatically unequal economic circumstances?

Perhaps the most important argument against a
democratic world state, however, is this: technically,
such a state would not be far removed from the aforementioned global dictatorship, because once it has
been possible to unite all the nations of the world into
a centrally administered unitary state, then any weakness in the leading institutions can be used to establish
a unified command system. Only a few adjustments
would have to be made. Anyone who has seen in
the last few years how quickly democratic states can
be transformed into authoritarian systems without
significant changes in their constitutional structures

must regard such a vision with fear and dread. And at the end of such a transformation there would be no available state to which freedom-loving people might still emigrate.

So there is a good side to the fact that a world government does not exist. And yet we feel its absence to the extent that the functions it would assume must be carried out. Who is responsible for the creation and preservation of global public goods? Who will ensure a healthy level of global redistribution between rich and poor? All of this requires coordination between the existing nation states. This coordination can take place "softly" or "informally"—for example through coordinated soft law—but it can also be reflected in hard treaties or even in the establishment of supranational institutions, and has been done so more and more over the past decades. Even if different degrees of firmness in the respective commitments are conceivable, the institutions responsible for compliance with these treaties usually lack something that might characterize a real central government, namely the ability of the military and/or police to exert "direct coercion." Quite independently of an underdeveloped system of sanctions, there is equally, however, a material difference between the contractual relationship in a confederation of states and institutional subjection in a federal state—treaties can be terminated.

Most recently, the Republican-led US government has shown how easy it is to legally dismantle a network of contractual obligations and erode highly sophisticated institutions such as the World Trade Organization by using delaying tactics.

This means that if there is no central global authority, we need other mechanisms to achieve political goals at a global level. These mechanisms must be designed to accommodate the interests of the individual states as they enter into and observe international treaty obligations. In economic terms, therefore, incentive compatibility is the order of the day. Whether the issue is global tax coordination by the OECD or the environmental goals of the Paris Agreement, states have to be persuaded to submit to these treaties in their own best interests and to uphold this commitment, even if it leads to domestic conflicts or competitive disadvantages internationally. In reality, this should work primarily when the reciprocal network of treaties between states has reached such a high degree of density that a calculated exit from a single treaty would cause such huge disadvantages to one particular state's position in the rest of the treaty network that the system creates its own stabilization. There are also disadvantages to this, however: in such a treaty network pertinent scientific problems and political solutions are, so to speak, permanently "frozen." The ability to adapt spontaneously to changing political challenges is weakened. It is no coincidence that countries such as the United Kingdom and the United States have sought an almost violent escape from long-term voluntary commitments in recent years in order to maintain their sovereign ability to act in the long run. The successful coordination mechanisms of the European internal market, which have been the basis of the European Union's economic prosperity for decades, can also be counterproductive as a result of overregulation and sclerosis. And state flexibility is needed not only to carry through changes in political preferences; we need it for the simple reason that reality can change in unforeseen ways.

This is where international competition comes into play, something that is not so easy in a globally coordinated world—and especially in one that is centrally controlled. Such competition between states should not (only) be imagined as a zero-sum game between strong and weak parties, in which fixed sums are shifted back and forth as profits. Regulatory competition between states is also—in Hayek's sense—a process of discovering better laws, a "noble competition" to find the appropriate solution to problems. As such, it fulfills two purposes that are difficult to achieve in a unitary world state. On the one hand, regulatory competition addresses the problem of information which necessarily accompanies and weakens a remote world government (even when benevolent) in its political activities. On the other hand, competition between states ensures that the individual citizen has the indispensable freedom to secure a better future for themselves personally by leaving for another territory and teaching the states involved a lesson "with their feet." Regulatory competition is thus to be understood not only instrumentally as an alternative legislative procedure. It is deeply connected with the personal freedom of the individual and the resulting fundamental right to emigrate based on human rights. The individual who is subject to a world government that has no need to fear competition will not be able to escape it anywhere on earth.

But how can we succeed in realizing important global goals in the institutional competition between states without incurring failures caused by the interventions of free-riders and obstructionists? A first step must be for democratic states to be sure of their own objectives. Is it just a question of increasing the prosperity and welfare of their own population? This is the traditional job description of state sovereigns, which Germany's Basic Law also includes in the oath of office sworn by the German Chancellor. Or are states in a position to include goals related to the global common good in how they act in the future? How far does the public spiritedness of individual communities extend?

Ultimately, the correct answer to this question does not primarily depend on the will or self-interest of the officials responsible. It is decided by the will and self-conception of the citizens who, as the "nation," sovereignly determine the main political trajectories of their country through elections and votes. Do the people of a nation feel solidarity with other nations? Does the individual see himself not just as part of a "global population", but also of a "global community"? And are the members of this global community prepared to share their sympathies and resources with all the other people who are, by a twist of fate, stuck on this planet? The theory of constitutional law is in no better position to teach us about this than are the axioms of political economy. The outcome can only emerge within the discourse of a global public sphere that extends beyond local and domestic (or even European) circles. The most recent experience of the COVID-19 pandemic might lead us to assume that in fundamental crises, in the end it's "every man for himself" and that the distinctions between "us" and "them" that for a long time had been considered over and done with were being drawn once again. But this doesn't have to be the last word. The decisive touchstone will be climate change, the consequences of which take place globally and the causes of which can only be combated globally.

Returning to our initial question, this means that the establishment of a world government is not to be expected, nor is it desired. But to create out of the peoples of the world a "global community" that has a sense of belonging and solidarity would be a huge step. It will not be possible to launch this development merely "from above," not just through the ideas and actions of institutions and elites. It must start in the minds of billions of world citizens who are not committed to narrow-minded nationalism, but also do not see themselves as rootless "citizens of nowhere," but rather as free citizens of a global community who care for one another. If this sense of self emerges, then we would have no need of a world government; instead, voluntary cooperation between sovereign states, energized by imaginative competition between different systems, can offer answers to our global questions.

CHAPTER 8

IF YOU WANT TO PREVENT A DEVASTATING WORST-CASE SCENARIO, ANTICIPATE IT

BAZON BROCK

In the esteemed Lübeck merchants' guildhall, a legend in calligraphy has proclaimed "since time immemorial" that people who trade with each other do not go to war. Even in June 1914, enlightened Humanists writing in liberal periodicals were captivated by the glad tidings that war was impossible in Europe because all potential adversaries were bound together by profound commercial relationships. And who would want to risk an ever-increasing economic benefit? Moreover, the argument went, the dynasties and nobility of

Europe—especially in Germany and England—were closely related by both blood and marriage. The aristocratic sentiment of blood ties actually turned out to be an emotional issue for the middle classes too—albeit in exactly the opposite way. For soon, in a way that seemed contrary to all economic sense, Europeans were hurtling towards each other in the name of the blood of their fatherlands.

Of course, every schoolchild could know that there is no such thing as pure blood in the Aryan or any other ancestral lineage. Unity through purity was and is a fantasy, a mere counterfactual. But all cultures derive their strength from recognizing the power of the counterfactual—the power of religions, world views, mythologies, epics, and fairy tales. The power of the counterfactual is the most important reality for any collective body and the culture it professes. Even if it is madness, it inevitably has a very strong impact. It is safe to say that the National Socialists' so-called "Parsifal laws" (Nuremberg Rally, 1935)[1] were the historical culmination of this, bearing in mind that in history there are no singularities, only norms. There is not the slightest doubt that "America First" or the Chinese quest for supremacy, like all nationalistic creeds, are still supported time and again by the cultural affinity of "us," even if we would like to believe that the flow of capital is more important than the flow of blood.

What is that supposed to mean? Capital interests do not conflict with nationalism. Supposedly hard economic facts do not contradict the magical powers of fairy tales and religions. After all, capitalism itself has become the greatest religion in the history of the world, and its global, fairy-tale-like powers work miracles that exceed all the wonders of history to an unimaginable degree. Since billions of dollars have been pouring into film, TV, or streaming productions every year, legends adapted to the modern world have been operating on a mass scale to underpin the belief in the wonderful world of consumerism—the universally disseminated vision of a life in paradise.

But how, in the worst-case scenarios of the culture wars, do we end up endangering or even destroying these miraculous beliefs? If capitalism is universally dominant, surely it would have to guarantee world peace out of its own economic interests, especially when peace means maintaining the effectiveness of capitalism—that is, the world's religion. How could that be achieved? By maintaining the balance of power between two forces: "bringing-into-the-world" by producing goods and "removing-from-the-world" the goods that have been produced by using them, consuming them, and creating waste. From a capitalist point of view, wars are required to continue producing all kinds of goods—weapons in particular. Classically, weapons as goods were a way of creating the means of consuming things radically and quickly, because destruction is the most powerful form of disposal and therefore required to keep the mass production of goods going.

But is the overall effect of weapons actually even greater than the effect of expiry dates, which are supposed to remove products from the world when they have not been used up? Less respectable businesspeople think that they worked out long ago how to significantly increase the turnover of goods. At the same time as selling the weapons, they sell a guarantee that the reconstruction of what has been destroyed will be secured by all economic means. It's a wonderful kind of reinsurance that means in effect that any actual traffic accident increases gross national product, and any kind of alternative energy guarantees the profitable continuation of business in the energy industry.

But if this is so, why do lots of people say that today's world is so unstable? The answer may still come as a surprise to the great thinkers in Europe. It is because the balance between "bringing-into-the-world" and "removing-from-the-world", which is necessary for maintaining capitalism, can no longer be guaranteed. The so-called climate crisis with all its ecological consequences is a clear example of this. The resources of creative production are simply not infinite, because even human ingenuity is limited by the laws of nature. Billions of years of evolution cannot be outweighed by a century of apparently limitless human creativity.

So we have to anticipate the devastating worst-case scenario—the failure of capitalism. Essentially, this means anticipating a rapid increase in re-nationalization and with it the basic decision of interest-based alliances to make the friend-enemy distinction. The most powerful such polarizations can be seen in the failure of capitalism embodied in the clashes between China, the USA, and Europe, countries whose own domestic cohesion is also threatened by the quest for supremacy among local religions and ethnic groups. To cope with this threat, power would have to be exercised in a way that would in any case largely run counter to democracies based on the rule of law and the welfare state. There would then remain the option of security over freedom, although, as history teaches us, security cannot be guaranteed in the longer term, even using the most rigorous measures.

Is there no solution, no chance, no way forward? There might be, at best, a postponement, if we manage to create an efficient kind of capitalism. This would mean finally re-establishing the market as a regulatory force, because the kind of capitalism we have known hitherto—not economic, but merely ideological capitalism—had, precisely through the use of subsidies and other negotiated interventions, deprived the market of the functional logic that might actually substantiate it. To date, economic capitalism has never existed, although a few illustrious capitalists have emerged here and there.

Note

1. The German Nazi Party's annual Nuremberg Rally [*Reichsparteitag*] in 1935 introduced the racist and anti-Semitic Nuremberg Laws: The Law for the Protection of German Blood and German Honor forbade marriages and extramarital intercourse between Jews and Germans, and the Reich Citizenship Law removed citizenship rights from all state subjects without German or related blood.

CHAPTER 9

COLLABORATION STRENGTHENS THE IMMUNE SYSTEM OF THE GLOBAL COMMUNITY

STEFAN OSCHMANN

"A complex functional system of an organism, which maintains bodily functions by warding off harmful or exogenous organisms."[1] This is how the legendary German medical reference work *Pschyrembel* describes the immune system. The immune system comprises various organs, cell types, and molecules, including the skin's natural barriers, mucous membranes, and various cells that recognize foreign objects and render them harmless, as well as the lymphatic system, the spleen, and bone marrow, which produce and transport these cells. All these elements work together very effectively to protect the body.

Why am I starting an article about collaboration with this—highly simplified—description of the immune system? Because evolution can teach us how completely different, highly specialized agents work in close harmony to deal with ever-changing challenges, thus ultimately allowing us to survive.

I am convinced that we also need this kind of complex, functional system in our connected world. After all, we are facing serious global risks and there is little that a single country or corporate group can do to combat them on its own. The COVID-19 pandemic has clearly underscored this. Climate change is another example. Using the analogy of the immune system, I consider it essential that we consciously combine our diverse strengths, perspectives, and methods to ensure healthy future prospects for everyone. In other words, as a global community, we need stronger multilateral solidarity that extends across national borders. And we need considerably more cross-sectoral partnerships between politics, science, business, and other areas, such as non-governmental organizations (NGOs) and foundations. The speed and severity of the COVID-19 pandemic has clearly exposed undesirable develop-ments as well as positive examples. What conclusions can be drawn for how we can sustainably develop our cooperation models further, particularly as regards public health?

SEIZING THE OPPORTUNITIES OF GLOBALIZATION

The key significance of internationally coordinated approaches quickly became clear at the start of the pandemic: as viruses effortlessly cross national borders, so too must our coordinated measures for fighting them. Against this background, the nationalist tendencies of the last few years are not a positive development. That is to say, we would be wise to once again make the benefits of globalization transparent and relatable to more people. Increasing global interconnectivity has led to greater production and productivity, created jobs, increased wages, and lowered prices—both in industrialized nations and poorer countries.[2] As a scientist, I would add that we now have unprecedented access to progress made around the world in technology and research. This also improves our lives. Thus, we ultimately benefit when the global community moves closer together.

It is precisely because of international collaboration in the health sector that we can promote prosperity and safety around the world. A key topic here is Universal Health Coverage, one of the development goals of the United Nations. At least half of the world's population currently has no access to basic healthcare. For ethical reasons alone, we have a responsibility to change this situation together.

At the same time, robust global healthcare will benefit us all. As regards the fight against the pandemic, COVID-19 has made it clear how crucial strong healthcare systems are for containing or, preferably, preventing these kinds of crises. The more unstable the supply structures of a region, the quicker the spread and the more dramatic the consequences. In specific terms, this means that during an epidemic, as a global community we are only as safe as the weakest country.

But even beyond that, we have much to gain as a global community by improving healthcare across the world. During the pandemic, we have all experienced how closely the development of the economy is connected to health matters. In fact, the McKinsey Global Institute has calculated that this effect is far greater than the presumed economic damage caused by COVID-19. According to this source, health-related problems depress GDP by around 15 percent every year. This is an enormous effect, which far exceeds the impact of COVID-19. Conversely, every

US dollar paid towards health could pay off two to four times over.[3] Global commitment to better healthcare is therefore a worthwhile goal in every respect. How do we make progress here?

I am firmly convinced that strong international organizations are a crucial success factor here. The World Health Organization (WHO) is the right agent to coordinate a global approach to health matters. In fact, WHO does outstanding work in many areas that we fundamentally rely on. However, it is also true that WHO has been massively weakened in recent years—both structurally and financially.[4] We now need to turn the tide. We must expand the resources and expertise of WHO and support them further. It must network even more effectively and develop further, especially as regards digitalization, then WHO can be the global hub for knowledge and measures for the better healthcare that we urgently need.

STRENGTHENING EUROPEAN SOLIDARITY

A strong Europe is also simply necessary in order to deal with complex challenges. The EU certainly has yet to make full use of its options in the face of the COVID-19 pandemic. At the same time, the many examples of European solidarity sent a clear positive signal at a time when too many nations were attempting to go it alone. Whether in regard to care of the sick, access to medical equipment, or economic aid for the Member States, after a few initial difficulties, the EU demonstrated in all these areas that it can be more than the sum of its parts.[5] When it comes to health issues in particular, this is especially important for many people. Should it prove possible to further expand cooperation in this area and to foster future-oriented sectors with the economic recovery plan in addition, then an opportunity will indeed arise for Europe to become a more important player on the international stage. A unified Europe can thus be a "healthy" Europe in many respects.

Accordingly, I very much welcome the fact that the EU is increasingly focusing on the value of intensive cooperation in the area of health issues. The EU4Health program, for example, is an effective initiative aimed at better preparing the European Union for health crises, improving coordination between the various Member States and ensuring that sufficient skilled personnel and equipment are available.[6]

Combining certain competencies at European level is also a positive step. This includes the plans to develop the European Centre for Disease Prevention and Control (ECDC) into an effective response center for international health crises. The establishment of a European version of BARDA,[7] the US authority for biomedical research and development, will also allow us to move forward. Such an authority will allow us to minimize cross-border risks and respond to emergencies more rapidly in the future.[8]

Now is a time when the EU can create positive impetus and provide a convincing model of how values-based international cooperation can work. The path is surely not an easy one, and uncertainty and populism are not making it any easier. In many cases, however, a foundation for potential success stories has already been laid.

A look at the highly dynamic European biotech scene shows this. I am convinced that as far as innovative companies in the health sector are concerned, Europe can further expand its leading position by taking the right measures. One important prerequisite is sound rules and regulations for handling data. With the General Data Protection Regulation (GDPR), the EU has set global standards with which other countries—from Chile to South Korea—are aligning their own approaches.[9] And indeed, these high data protection standards may prove to be an advantage for Europe as regards new businesses models relating to healthcare in particular. After all, hardly any information is more sensitive than information relating to health.

Therefore, we also need clear ethical guidelines, particularly in the medical sector, governing how we deal with data and algorithms worldwide. This is especially important for Merck as a healthcare company engaged in research. Because one key factor on which our success depends is the trust placed in us by our diverse range of stakeholders, from patients to public authorities to society as a whole. At the same time, global companies like Merck can observe on a daily basis the fatal impact of an international patchwork of ethical standards, both on medical advances and on competitiveness.

Europe can lead the way here with targeted proposals. And we have even greater potential: the centralized health systems in Europe constitute a valuable data pool. If we can find ways to evaluate this data in an anonymized and secure manner, it can enable enormous advances in the development of new therapies, for example in the fight against cancer. The fact that the EU aims to make the years from now until 2030 a "digital decade," with massive investments in joint data rooms, artificial intelligence, and the necessary infrastructure, is an important step that is being taken at the right time.[10]

A further approach that would make sense is the targeted promotion of a European ecosystem for innovation. Europe has numerous outstanding research institutions, highly innovative companies, and well-educated young talent. We should make the most of these valuable assets. This calls for competition law that looks beyond the European market and does not stand in the way of the emergence of global champions from Europe. It would also make sense to facilitate investments in startups in the areas of technology and research, particularly at a time when it is becoming increasingly difficult for young, highly innovative companies to find financing. According to a study, 70 percent of German startups have reported that the COVID-19 pandemic is threatening their existence.[11]

Moreover, in countries such as the United States or Israel we can see that an intensive dialogue between science, business, and government is an especially promising approach for establishing a stable culture of innovation. In Germany and in Europe, I often have the impression that, in this regard, we still need to break down barriers and reduce hesitance. This brings me to the second group of models that we need for a positive future: cooperation across different sectors.

BREAKING DOWN BARRIERS BETWEEN SECTORS

One perfect example of how much this approach can achieve does indeed come from Europe, namely the Innovative Medicines Initiative (IMI). This initiative is the world's largest public–private partnership in biosciences. The EU and the European pharmaceutical industry have already jointly provided more than €5 billion in this area, with the funds going primarily to projects at the precompetitive stage, i.e. basic research.[12] This approach has proven highly successful. Projects supported by the IMI have resulted in the identification of biomarkers and the development of vaccines against the Ebola virus. Similarly, the IMI is also supporting research on the COVID-19 pandemic. CARE, a consortium founded for this purpose, of which Merck is a member, is dedicated to seeking treatment methods for COVID-19 and has the long-term goal of expanding our knowledge of the disease.

Indeed, dealing with COVID-19 is demonstrating in many ways the value of having different sectors combine their strengths, starting with pandemic prevention. The fact *that* the likelihood of pandemics is growing has been apparent to many experts for a long time now. This is related to factors such as increasing urbanization, climate change, and the interconnectedness of global societies as well as under-developed healthcare systems in many regions of the world. The question of *how* we best prepare for these kinds of events is clearly still a matter for debate.

One initial pioneering result of such discussions came in 2017 with the Coalition for Epidemic Preparedness Innovations (CEPI). CEPI is a public–private partnership made up of governments, foundations, research institutions, and pharmaceutical companies, which aims to accelerate vaccine development. Indeed, the development of a vaccine against the SARS-CoV-2 virus highlights in many ways how different sectors work in close coordination and thus achieve advances at an unprecedented speed:[13]

• Governments and public authorities are taking on a coordinating role. They ensure that the usual stringent requirements have been met before a product is approved and they support the development of vaccines with public funds.[14] A further important task is then the distribution of the vaccine. This refers both to the distribution to various countries and the question of which sections of the population are to be immunized at what point in time. International collaboration on these matters is one of the core competencies of WHO, supported by organizations such as GAVI, the Vaccine Alliance. One particular key focus is to prevent individual governments from procuring vaccines exclusively for their own countries.

- The research institutions focus on advancing scientific knowledge about the virus and the disease that it causes. The extremely steep learning curve is related, not least, to how willingly and comprehensively new insights are shared around the globe. In this regard, cooperation in the context of the pandemic takes on an entirely new quality. Based on the insights they gain, companies and research institutions seek vaccine candidates.

- NGOs and foundations, such as the Bill & Melinda Gates Foundation, can send important signals by, for example, putting neglected topics on the agenda, giving underrepresented groups a voice, and initiating new alliances. Moreover, they can support countries in specific areas where certain structures are lacking.

Overall, this coordinated allocation of tasks is achieving impressive results. Normally, the overall process of developing a new vaccine takes about seven years.

In the case of the COVID-19 pathogen, authorities worldwide received the first applications for approval of vaccines after only a few months.

In fact, many initiatives that serve the greater good can benefit from close coordination between different sectors. One aspect of entrepreneurial thinking, for example, is defining clear goals and achieving them with a certain budget within a defined period of time. This practical orientation and the financial resources that companies have at their disposal can play a decisive role in driving project success.[15]

Conversely, how does it benefit companies to get involved above and beyond their core business? The list is long and goes far beyond merely enhancing their corporate image. The success of a leading science and technology company is, for example, inextricably linked to a high degree of motivation among its employees. Companies have been shown to achieve better results when they clearly define the contribution that they want to make to society. At Merck, we formulate this *purpose* as: "We are curious minds dedicated to human progress." We work on technological progress that benefits everyone. Moreover, the above-mentioned studies on the major impact of health on economic development show that companies benefit from improved social framework conditions.

And if we drive basic research within the scope of CEPI, for example, it ultimately boosts our own innovative power.

SECURING THE FUTURE TOGETHER

Accordingly, Merck participates in a large number of public–private projects, including in the context of the COVID-19 pandemic. Our Healthcare business sector, for example, donated a proven multiple sclerosis medicine to WHO for a study investigating its possible use for treating COVID-19. Within the scope of the CARE consortium, we are helping to accelerate research and development as regards the coronavirus. We are working with the Bill & Melinda Gates Foundation for this purpose as well.

And indeed, long before the pandemic, our experience was that public–private partnerships have many advantages, particularly in the area of healthcare. Together with other pharmaceutical companies and in collaboration with WHO and the Bill & Melinda Gates Foundation, we have taken up the fight against so-called neglected tropical diseases, which have a very negative impact on development in certain regions of the world. Merck is pursuing the goal of eliminating schistosomiasis, an insidious parasitic infection, which claims approximately 200,000 lives every year. We donate up to 250 million praziquantel tablets every year for this purpose. Together with partners, we are also currently researching a new formulation of the active ingredient for children under six years of age. In addition, we support the expansion and maintenance of infrastructure for sanitary facilities and invest in educational projects on health in the affected regions.

A further example is the AMR Action Fund, to which more than 20 pharmaceutical companies have donated a total of US$1 billion. Thanks to these funds, novel antibiotics are to emerge by 2030. The concept was developed together with WHO and the European Investment Bank—and there is a serious background to this. More and more bacteria are becoming resistant to existing antibiotics, which already results in about 700,000 deaths per year. If we do not act soon, this number could increase rapidly, especially since we rely on concomitant treatment with effective antibiotics for a variety of medical therapies. Paradoxically, however, there is no viable market for new products because in order to maintain their effectiveness, antibiotics are used as little as possible. This fact has already driven several smaller companies focusing on the development of new antibiotics into bankruptcy. No single country or organization can solve this complex problem alone. Therefore, the AMR Action Fund helps to close the current funding gap, thus giving lawmakers time to develop suitable market instruments to counteract the causes on a long-term basis.

In summary, all these examples show that we can only tackle the multifaceted challenges of our time together—because they affect us all in a great variety of ways, regardless of where we live and regardless of what sector we operate in. The COVID-19 pandemic has made this interdependence particularly percep- tible. This raises the question of lessons we can learn for dealing with other global crises—just think of climate change.

Personally, I have no doubt: just as we all have a certain responsibility for the health of others in these times, each and every individual should also make a contribution towards sustaining the basis of life on our planet. This also applies to each and every company. I think that the pandemic can, in fact, give us a certain amount of hope as regards mastering the climate crisis and tackling other Herculean tasks, because we see that trust in research and science has been growing during this time. And, with regard to climate change, I firmly believe that a strategy of just doing nothing will not get us any further. We need "technologies for the future"—innovative technologies that can slow down or even reverse global warming.

If we succeed in combining the positive force of research and development together with that of partners from all sectors and around the world, then the complex, functional immune system itself will emerge that the global community urgently needs to remain healthy over the long term.

Notes

1. Pschyrembel Online, *Immunsystem*, August 2020, https://www.pschyrembel.de/immunsystem/K0AMH/doc (accessed November 9, 2020).

2. Interview with Gita Gopinath, "An Economist explains the Pros and Cons of Globalization," World Economic Forum, April 11, 2019, https://www.weforum.org/agenda/2019/04/an-economist-explains-the-pros-and-cons-of-globalization-b2f0f4ae76 (accessed November 9, 2020).

3. McKinsey Global Institute, *Prioritizing Health: A Prescription for Prosperity*, July 2020, https://www.mckinsey.com/industries/healthcare-systems-and-services/our-insights/prioritizing-health-a-prescription-for-prosperity (accessed November 9, 2020).

4. Uta Steinwehr, "The World Health Organization in Crisis Mode," *Deutsche Welle*, May 18, 2020, https://www.dw.com/de/die-weltgesundheitsorganisation-im-krisenmodus/a-53473614 (accessed November 9, 2020).

5. European Commission, "Corona Crisis: European Solidarity in Action," https://ec.europa.eu/info/live-work-travel-eu/health/coronavirus-response/coronavirus-european-solidarity-action_de (accessed November 9, 2020).

6. European Commission, "Questions and Answers on the New EU4Health Program," May 28, 2020, https://ec.europa.eu/commission/presscorner/detail/de/QANDA_20_956 (accessed November 9, 2020).

7. Biomedical Advanced Research and Development Authority (BARDA).

8. State of the Union Address by Ursula von der Leyen, President of the European Commission, September 16, 2020, https://ec.europa.eu/commission/presscorner/detail/ov/SPEECH_20_1655 (accessed November 9, 2020).

9. Alexander Fanta, "DSGVO: Starkes Gesetz, holprige Durchsetzung" in *Netzpolitik*, June 24, 2020, https://netzpolitik.org/2020/starkes-gesetz-holprige-durchsetzung (accessed November 9, 2020); Europäische Kommission, "Gemeinsame Erklärung zum 2. Jahrestag der Datenschutzgrundverordnung," https://ec.europa.eu/commission/presscorner/detail/de/statement_20_913 (accessed November 9, 2020).

10. State of the Union Address by Ursula von der Leyen, President of the European Commission.

11. Bundesverband Deutsche Startups e.V., "Startup Association presents COVID-19 Study—Seven out of Ten Startups fear for their Existence," March 2020, https://deutschestartups.org/2020/03/31/startup-verband-legt-corona-studie-vor-jedes-siebte-startup-fuerchtet-um-die-existenz (accessed November 9, 2020).

12. Innovative Medicines Initiative, https://www.imi.europa.eu (accessed November 9, 2020).

13. Die Bundesregierung, "Das ist der Stand der Impfstoffforschung," November 4, 2020, https://www.bundesregierung.de/breg-de/themen/coronavirus/coronavirus-impfung-1788988 (accessed November 9, 2020).

14. Die Bundesregierung, "Impfstoff-Förderung angelaufen," September 15, 2020, https://www.bundesregierung.de/breg-de/themen/themenseite-forschung/corona-impfstoff-1787044 (accessed November 9, 2020).

15. Mark R. Kramer and Marc W. Pfitzer, "The Ecosystem of Shared Value" in *Harvard Business Review*, October 2016, https://hbr.org/2016/10/the-ecosystem-of-shared-value (accessed November 9, 2020).

CHAPTER 10

THE COMMON GOOD ON THE MOVE: THE PANDEMIC AS A CATALYST

TIMO MEYNHARDT

"One thing the coronavirus crisis has already proved is that there really is such a thing as society."[1] British Prime Minister Boris Johnson is stating the obvious: it only works if we work together; collective survival requires solidarity and the cooperation of everyone. Saying this at the start of the COVID-19 pandemic in March 2020, Johnson was, however, also setting something in motion that can be seen as an intellectual turning point whose outcome is open-ended.

Let's take a look back. In a 1987 interview, the then British Prime Minister Margaret Thatcher came out with the now notorious sentence, "There is no such thing as society." Taken out of the context of a much more nuanced interview, this sentence became the hallmark of her term of office and shorthand for a shift of emphasis towards more personal responsibility by the individual and away from state support. Depending on one's ideological orientation, this basic notion became a component of political programs and continues to have an impact today.

Thatcher would most certainly not agree with every way her words have been interpreted. However, one thing can be said of her: she was firmly convinced that the common good (she called it the "flourishing society") would be best served if everyone took responsibility for themselves and their immediate environment. The pandemic is now revealing the complexity of such a liberal perspective.

Already we can foresee that the effects of the pandemic will affect society as a whole and not just individual areas. New constellations of the common good will emerge which, in the best case scenario, are making society as a whole more resilient, more resistant, and more viable. In this essay, I would like to highlight the initiatives serving thinking about the common good that are already emerging from the pandemic and how they can be used productively.

WHAT THE PANDEMIC SHOWS

The first year of the COVID-19 crisis clearly shows us (once again) how dependent we all are on a functioning community. The idea of the autonomous individual who pursues their goals and takes responsibility for themselves and others turns out to be unsustainable if the necessary conditions for mutual dependency are not observed. This indeed is the legitimate reproach laid against the kind of individualism that insists on civil liberties above all without recognizing and appreciating the social forms of association ("sociality") on which they are based.

Infections reveal the quality of relationships ("forms of association") in the family, at work, or in public life, experienced as positive and negative dependencies, in a way that is as banal as it is brutal, simply through the danger posed by the air we share. We are existentially dependent on clean air to breathe and thus on minimizing the likelihood of airborne virus transmission. Nobody has "sovereignty over the air"—we are all connected to one another on a biological level via the air we breathe, even before we have exchanged a single word. The air we breathe is always social air. It feels like a drastic change in all areas of life when we have to reduce the amount of shared air that we usually breathe. Greater physical distances lead to greater social distances, which sometimes require a great deal of adaptation and have a powerful impact on our social life together.

No matter how we interpret our changed, distanced relationships, no one can deny the realization, which has been highlighted once again due to the new conditions affecting our air, of how complex our modern way of life is and how much we depend on others. Without a reliable framework, to which we ourselves contribute through our own actions (even if it is "only" the clearly understood self-interest of physical distancing), it is inconceivable that we might exercise our individual aspirations to freedom.

Becoming aware of our own vulnerability is an essential moment in our totally subjective experience of why our own wellbeing depends on and in turn influences the wellbeing of others. None of us can survive in an airless space, literally or figuratively, and everyone contributes to filling the "vacuum." This systemic dependence on one another, which lies beyond our personal desires, often surpasses our faculties of perception. Therefore, many people find it hard to acknowledge the functional importance of social forms of association (including their biological preconditions) as a premise of individual freedoms. For such people, it only becomes apparent during a crisis how any form of self-realization through the experience of autonomy, self-control, and self-efficacy turns out to be the fragile result of a thoroughly collective effort: without the common good there is no freedom, without "we" there is no "I"—we "are" only through and with other people. I think this eye-opening experience of the primacy of the social element is the main message behind Boris Johnson's comment, and less a question of the role of the state and the responsibility of the individual.

THE RENAISSANCE OF THINKING ABOUT THE COMMON GOOD

Thinking about the common good is undergoing a resurgence, and not just since the onset of the current pandemic. Since the financial crisis of 2008/09 and with the emergence of increasingly significant climate scenarios, individualistic ways of thinking have taken a knock-back. The COVID-19 crisis gives a much more powerful, perhaps even abrupt, twist to focusing on the common good.

This might even shake up the most recent answers to the question of the common good to the same extent that the 1755 Lisbon earthquake spurred philosophers into new and different ways of thinking about the role of human beings in their forms of association with the world. In the 21st century it is no longer predominantly a question of how a benevolent God could allow a disaster to happen (the theodicy problem). Today the question is how should modern, open societies respond to crises that can only be surmounted by massively restricting personal freedom. In these circumstances, how can we conceive of the relationship between the common good and freedom?

The common good does not contradict the freedom of us all, both individually and collectively, but constitutes its premise—in the spirit of the Second Vatican Council, where the common good was understood as "the sum of those conditions of the social life whereby men, families and associations more adequately and readily may attain their own perfection."[2]

In addition to this systemic perspective, there is the quotidian view, according to which the experience of the common good is to be understood as

> ...general social experience in the form of intuitive knowledge about social conditions [...]. The common good is important for each of us because we cannot simply invent a world, but already live under conditions which are in many ways important to us all. The

common good also lies, so to speak, in the framework that is created collectively. These are conditions in a realm of relationships that lend direction and structure to our identity and personal narratives.[3]

However, this basic and fundamental liberal tradition of thought has not had an easy time over the last few decades, when skepticism about the common good was on the rise. As a result of lessons learned from the experience of the Third Reich, the baby was often thrown out with the bathwater and what was originally well-considered caution was unabashedly freighted with accusations of authoritarianism (primarily citing Carl Schmitt's dictum: "Anyone who speaks of the *bonum commune* is intent on deception"[4]). In tandem with the advance of functional differentiation, the core of thinking about the common good is being hollowed out more and more, apparently evaporating into individual lifestyles ("singularities").[5]

Whether in today's wave of privatizing public services, in attempts at administrative reform, or in the business world, people everywhere thought that the common good was most likely to be served when economic and, in particular, competitive factors took effect. If everyone thinks of themselves, everyone is taken care of—this was the mantra in the tradition of Adam Smith, the Scottish moral philosopher whose view was quite unjustly abbreviated to the phrase the "invisible hand" of market forces. Those who rejected the common good no longer saw any unifying systemically relevant qualities in modern society and even wanted to philosophize any obligation to the common good out of the economy. This is likely to prove short-sighted.

The *Public Value Atlas*, a representative survey of public value issues, regularly illustrates the role played by questions of the common good among the population. For example, in 2019, 81 percent of respondents in Germany were concerned that the common good was not receiving enough attention in the country.[6] The need to take a closer look once again at what connects society is by no means a purely academic debate.

BEYOND THE PRIORITIES OF DIFFERENTIATION THEORY: REVERSING THE POINT OF DEPARTURE

Are doubts now setting in? We must look for answers in the way we live together, leading us straight away to the question of the common good that must be answered not in heaven but here on earth. What is at issue is nothing less than a reversal of the point of departure, which says that it is not functional differentiation but rather social forms of association that create the basis of the modern community. It is the quality of the forms of association between people on which every social order is built and from which it draws its legitimizing power. This is where the necessary support comes from that makes a social order viable in the first place. We are now seeing how much, for example, our economic system depends on these forms of association and cannot function without them.

Mutual social affirmation, the primacy of the social element, is itself based on psychological and, as we are now realizing, even biological forms of association, which make us dependent on one another to a much greater extent than we might like. The social element creates the framework in which forms of individuality can develop in the first place.

We can therefore assume that COVID-19 is accelerating the moment when differentiation theories will come to an end and integration theories will enjoy a renaissance. In the latter, societies are described less on the basis of differentiations, singularities, or intrinsic logics, but rather, and more powerfully, on the basis of the forms of association that shape them. We can now clearly see something of which we had not been reminded for a long time: we must be able to afford types of differentiation. When they become too dominant and undermine what unites us, the common good suffers.

In reversing the point of departure, another notion comes into play: dedifferentiation means going back to more general questions of association and thereby a reduction in complexity. According to the developmental psychology of Jean Piaget, this interplay of differentiation and dedifferentiation requires a dynamic balance between the classification of new experiences in existing worldviews (assimilation) and changes to this worldview itself brought about by new experiences (accommodation).[7] The "impositions" of diverse perspectives in the modern age[8] require completely new forms of accommodation to process complexity and simplification. Previous differentiations are integrated at a new level into the resulting new condition. What seemed difficult and complicated before suddenly becomes understandable in a new light and reveals an internal order, for example a pattern, a rule, or a system. This basic mechanism, described by Piaget in terms of developmental psychology, is necessary in order to bring the abundance of different perspectives into a coherent context, without which purposive action is impossible. Dedifferentiation offers the opportunity of striking out on new paths where egregious paradoxes and dilemmas seem to offer no way out.

Fraught with impositions, these differentiation tendencies will otherwise quickly overwhelm the human ability to deal with a diversity of perspectives, and prove to be confusing. Even more important for thinking about the common good, however, is the concealment of fundamental mutual dependencies linked to the differentiation discourse, as the pandemic has reminded us. This is not a plea to abandon the differentiation debate because of an existential threat that is teaching us to focus on "the essentials." Rather it is about promoting a form of accommodation so that all actors can take part in the common good on an equal footing.

We might even say it is a new look at what Friedrich Hölderlin called the only "dispute in the world": "namely what has priority, the whole or the individual." How thinking about the common good will actually refocus itself remains to be seen. The desire to use the crisis to press one's own convictions as to what constitutes the common good (for example, climate change or globalization) is certainly legitimate. This is easier to do in one's individual life than in a complex society. For example, not taking a cruise is easier than implementing new kinds of ship propulsion systems in the entire industry.

One lesson can already be drawn, however: one reason why thinking about the common good has become important again lies in the new sensitivity towards vulnerability in general. This does not mean hypersensitivity to attacks on identity as a result of otherness or experiences of foreignness, but rather a new awareness of the fundamental precariousness of life.[9] By becoming aware of their own vulnerability, the individual has the opportunity of recognizing their fundamental dependence on others. This ethic of vulnerability is at the same time an ethic of the common good, as reflected in the debate about society's "vulnerable groups," who require special protection against the virus.

Focusing on vulnerability as a universal condition of existence and thus a principle of the common good contains a great opportunity beyond identity politics and towards a new kind of solidarity, a modern form of compassion and thus towards a new kind of liberalism, in which people's potential for development is regarded primarily independent of origin and ethnicity. This return to "being human" itself would in this case bring unexpected progress in terms of the common good, which in turn allows new differentiations and perspectives. In this way, modern society, with its high level of functional differentiation, is once again becoming aware of its basis in the common good, something it seemed to be losing sight of.

AGGREGATE STATES OF THE COMMON GOOD

During the COVID-19 pandemic, when the air quality became significant in a new and literally existential way, describing the common good as shared air that does not belong to any one person, to which everyone contributes, which everyone can pollute or keep clean, turns out to be just as useful as a general way of describing the social and dynamic nature of the common good. There is a good reason why we use metaphorical formulations in everyday language such as "up in the air," "clearing the air," or "disappearing into thin air."

To distinguish between what is just "hot air" in the coming debates and where something is really on the move, it is worthwhile returning to the notion of the aggregate states of various types of public opinion as described by Ferdinand Tönnies,[10] one of the founding fathers of sociology. This can be linked to the useful idea of conceiving the rise and fall of belief in the common good as a process.

Applying Tönnies' notion to the common good, we can distinguish three types that differ in terms of how binding they are: solid common good (for example, the principle of democracy), fluid common good (for example, debates about new kinds of citizen participation), and gaseous common good (for example, the influence of social media on collective decision-making). This refers to more or less binding values, rules and norms, depending on the aggregate state. In a liberal, open society, the common good must keep moving and allow phase transitions in all directions, as long as these can be justified within the constitutional system or lead to an amendment of the system.

While in normal times we can concern ourselves more with air-like and fluid forms of the common good and can cultivate (subtle) differences, in times of crisis the common good's more solid components come to the fore all the more significantly. Are they sustainable or are they built on sand? Does the suspension of legally inscribed beliefs in the common good, even if temporary, destroy their inner affirmation? What happens if what has thus far been taken for granted in terms of individual freedom turns out to be counterproductive for collective survival?

When survival is at stake, broadly accepted and stable foundations of the common good, without which we cannot afford to make superficial differentiations (singularities, filter bubbles, echo chambers), are important. Conversely, the exaggeration of individual values that are seemingly set in stone harbors the very risk of their destruction. The end has never sanctified the means. Now it becomes clear what is really happening with the common good, whether the fractured routines of everyday life in partnerships, families, businesses, and offices will once again ultimately reassert themselves in all areas of coexistence, or whether irreversible changes will occur, creating completely different forms of association and, as a result, constellations of the common good.

It is thus unclear whether the new technological forms of interaction resulting from necessity will solidify or are merely a temporary liquefaction of previously loose obligations. By far the greatest endurance test for the common good, however, is likely to be the question of whether the discrepancies between the socially, culturally, and economically privileged and everyone else, which may have worsened as a result of the crisis, will lead to dissatisfaction, social conflict, and alienation, which will in turn set things in motion and shake up the situation.

TIMO MEYNHARDT

The above example of changes in collective decision-making (the principle of democracy, new kinds of citizen participation, influence of social media on collective decision-making) is a question that concerns altered constellations of the common good: that is, the potential to mediate between the satisfaction of individual needs and a functioning community with regard to participation and involvement in social processes.

Questioning constellations of the common good in terms of their aggregate state has a very practical value: readers of this essay might read a comment about political, economic, cultural, or social issues in a daily newspaper and can try to identify the common good in its solid, fluid, and gaseous components. In many cases this process will prove an illuminating way of identifying possible developments in the common good.

The challenge is to validate changes in the aggregate states of the common good as contributions to a functioning, living community. When it comes to the issue of the common good, decision-makers are responsible for carefully weighing up where they want to make cuts or where to consolidate. The great achievement in interpretation and, consequently, in leadership consists in the ability to seek the common good in the concrete, but not to confuse the two. As a "necessary fiction," the experience of the common good inevitably transcends the facts at hand; it cannot be derived directly from them.[11] The "facts" must first be scrutinized notionally in terms of their possible experience as a form of the common good. This consists in an inner affirmation or rejection of social facts. Ascribing a value to the common good is in no way a random or even arbitrary process, if we take the idea of the primacy of the social element seriously and see subjective evaluations themselves as expressions of social processes through which the individual has internalized social values and norms.

This paradox of the so-called immanent transcendence of the common good can be summed up thus: "To understand the common good as a category of experience of the social element inevitably means relying on the individual's skills in perception, indeed ultimately being obliged to rely on them. This does not mean just sensory impressions, but rather the ability to translate one's own experiences in the social world into a subjective context of needs and to classify them emotionally."[12]

In the acute COVID-19 crisis, as we have already mentioned, our own vulnerability and the connection between individual and collective survival are the key to the relevance of the common good. After the crisis, other views about its relevance will return to prominence, as the historical analysis of past pandemics suggests.[13]

THE COMMON GOOD IN A POST-PANDEMIC WORLD

Data collected in summer 2020—the first year of the pandemic—shows that the COVID-19 crisis is changing the public's awareness of the common good. For example, 60 percent of those surveyed state that the common good has become more important to them.[14] It remains to be seen whether this effect will last.

In many instances, commentators are already seeing the pandemic acting as a catalyst, enabling new developments or accelerating those that are already emerging and steering them in a certain direction. Is humanity once again facing a fundamental change—a *metanoia*—that will lead to a good life in community and society?

For decision-makers in business, politics, and society, an injection of dynamism into the common good is both an opportunity and a risk. Arguments about public tolerance, public benefit, or innovation for the common good, as well as harm and damage to the common good, lend themselves well to legitimizing or delegitimizing complex decisions. There is no doubt that these ways of facilitating or even burdening this reasoning will determine important debates in the public realm over the next few years. The deeper reason for this lies in the integrative power of thinking about the common good in order to overcome emerging contradictions and paradoxes by shifting to another level of reference. The recipe for success is not yet more reflection, but an attractive combination of thoughtful reflection and emotional appeal. The common good can never be true or false; it is always about the enactment of certain values that prove themselves subjectively and receive collective affirmation.

In times of crisis, despite all the mobility inherent in the common good, enlightened Europe always stands at a crossroads where there can be only one compass, namely the inviolability of the dignity of the individual. In this respect, the moment has now come for liberal philosophers of the common good—those who can turn the conditions for the free development of each individual and therefore everyone into an intellectual principle. The question of the common good is becoming the ultimate liberal issue.

Notes

1. Boris Johnson, video message, https://t.co/kxdqItMYSE, Twitter, March 29, 2020 (accessed February 8, 2021).

2. Second Vatican Council: *Gaudium et spes*, Chapter IV: The Life of the Political Community, para. 74, 1966. http://www.vatican.va/archive/hist_councils/ii_vatican_council/documents/vat-ii_cons_19651207_gaudium-et-spes_en.html (accessed January 13, 2021).

3. Timo Meynhardt, "Ohne Gemeinwohl keine Freiheit: Zur Psychologie des Gemeinwohls" in Hans-Jürgen Papier and Timo Meynhardt (eds.) *Freiheit und Gemeinwohl: Ewige Gegensätze oder zwei Seiten einer Medaille* (Berlin: Tempus Corporate, 2016), p. 188.

4. Quoted in Josef Isensee, *Gemeinwohl und öffentliches Amt. Vordemokratische Fundamente des Verfassungsstaates* (Wiesbaden: Springer VS, 2013), p. 39.

5. Andreas Reckwitz, *Die Gesellschaft der Singularitäten: Zum Strukturwandel der Moderne* (Berlin: Suhrkamp Verlag, 2018).

6. www.gemeinwohlatlas.de/en (accessed February 8, 2021).

7. Jean Piaget, *The Origin of Intelligence in the Child* (London: Taylor & Francis, 2013).

8. Peter Strohschneider, *Zumutungen: Wissenschaft in Zeiten von Populismus, Moralisierung und Szientokratie* (Hamburg: kursbuch.edition, 2020).

9. Judith Butler, *Precarious Life: The Powers of Mourning and Violence* (London/New York: Verso, 2004).

10. *Ferdinand Tönnies on Public Opinion: Selections and Analyses*, edited, introduced and translated by Hanno Hardt and Slavko Splichel (Lanham: Rowman and Littlefield, 2000).

11. Timo Meynhardt, "Public Value Inside: What is Public Value Creation?" in *International Journal of Public Administration*, vol. 32, issues 3–4 (2009), pp. 192–219.

12. Timo Meynhardt, "Ohne Gemeinwohl keine Freiheit: Zur Psychologie des Gemeinwohls," p. 180.

13. Laura Spinney, *Pale Rider: The Spanish Flu of 1918 and How it Changed the World* (London: Jonathan Cape, 2017).

14. www.gemeinwohlatlas.de/en (accessed February 8, 2021).

CHAPTER 11

THE RETURN OF RAPPROCHEMENT IN EUROPE

CHRISTOPH G. PAULUS

1. THE POINT OF DEPARTURE

The following remarks do not advance a new alliance for the present moment, but rather argue in favor of renewing an existing alliance, which is urgently needed in the present author's opinion. In doing so, our discussion will refer to observations made by the author in last year's Convoco! Edition, which aimed to demonstrate the value of Europe's diversity.[1] Today, by contrast, we will discuss the quest for how one can preserve what has been achieved or even strengthen it when it is threatening collapse.

To ensure a better understanding, let us briefly recapitulate. As we know, the history of Europe is drenched in blood. As if trying to prove Heraclitus' dictum that war is the father of all things, for almost two millennia the European states took every opportunity—real or simply hyped-up—to attack each other. Looked at microscopically, this attitude can be seen throughout the 30 years of the war whose name refers purely to this period of time. Even today it is still questionable whether just one war took place between 1618 and 1648 or a group of wars, because many rulers once again took the opportunity to fight each another, and— because in any case it was already a battlefield— to do it on the territory of the German states. Even external enemies—the Mongols or the Ottomans, for example—were unable to alter the mutually hostile attitude of the Europeans and bring about a closing of ranks—albeit only temporarily—between the states.

This sad but in reality horrific situation went hand in hand with all the cultural achievements that make up the European heritage, the list of which, as we know, goes well beyond the Renaissance and the cuckoo clock.[2] But in an ever more densely populated world, we certainly should not want to resign ourselves to this antagonism between culture and war; that would be playing with fire at a time when even the smallest conflicts anywhere on the globe have the potential more and more often to trigger a world war. Consequently, it was World War II that, for the first time in history, prompted European heads of state to seriously consider and move forward with an unwarlike coexistence on this continent. That was the prelude to the European Treaties, the authors of which proceeded sensibly enough, not striving for a uniform structure, but rather, as De Gaulle put it at the time, for a "Europe of the fatherlands." One should not be made out of many (as per the motto of the United States of America), but rather people wanted to be united in diversity.

2. THE FIRST SOLUTION AND ITS DIMINISHING ATTRACTIVENESS

From a legal perspective, we should stress that this revolutionary step not only required the determination of great politicians who were also big thinkers, but also these politicians had to employ a legal set of instruments to achieve their aims—namely treaties. Accordingly, treaties [*Verträge*] were instrumentalized in their literal sense; the *Vertrag* and its corresponding verb *sich vertragen* [to get along with] both include the sense of peace-making. This is even more evident in its Latin counterpart *pactum* and the associated verb *pacisci* [to pacify, to make peace].

This etymology is more than just an intellectual game; rather it is an agenda to ensure that there should never again be war among European neighbors. The previous 30 years or so (that period again) had led not only the continent but virtually the whole world to the edge of the abyss. The horror had been experienced by everyone directly, and was deeply imprinted on the body and soul of all who had lived through it. That is why the preamble to the Treaty establishing the European Economic Community says:

> RESOLVED to strengthen the safeguards of peace and liberty by establishing this combination of resources, and calling upon the other peoples of Europe who share their ideal to join in their efforts...

This statement can hardly be surpassed in terms of significance: in absolutely diametrical contrast with the previous experience of war and subjugation, the lofty goal of peace and liberty was to be achieved through the Treaties, with the union of economic forces serving as the driver—coalition rather than competition, cooperation instead of parallel or conflicting interests. Even more clearly than in the EEC Treaty, which came into force in 1957, the attempt to transform the warlike past into a peaceful future by bringing together economic powers is expressed in the Preamble to the European Coal and Steel Community. In this Treaty, which took effect in 1952, it says:

CONSIDERING that world peace can be safeguarded only by creative efforts commensurate with the dangers that threaten it,

CONVINCED that the contribution which an organized and vital Europe can make to civilization is indispensable to the maintenance of peaceful relations,

RECOGNIZING that Europe can be built only through practical achievements which will first of all create real solidarity, and through the establishment of common bases for economic development,

ANXIOUS to help, by expanding their basic production, to raise the standard of living and further the works of peace,

RESOLVED to substitute for age-old rivalries the merging of their essential interests; to create, by establishing an economic community, the basis for a broader and deeper community among peoples long divided by bloody conflicts; and to lay the foundations for institutions which will give direction to a destiny henceforward shared...

Even more directly than in the later Treaty, history is referred to in this Treaty—in its bloody and destructive guise as well as in its civilizing aspect—in order to introduce and justify the change of course and to establish its necessity. The Treaties (as we know, the Euratom Treaty is the third in the group) actually saw themselves in the literal sense as bringers of peace, and that is still part of their narrative.

Now, a narrative almost always has two sides; one positive, the other not necessarily negative, but less positive. The positive side of a narrative—or founding myth—condenses the initial circumstances underlying the establishment of the narrative (in this case the foundation of a European Community) in an easily comprehensible, catchy, and communicable way. What could be more convincing and urgent for those who survived the recent horror than peace at last after literally thousands of years of war?

The less positive side of this narrative emerges, on the one hand, from its all too palatable urgency and, on the other hand, from its dependence on outlook and experience. As far as the former is concerned, the grand, meaningful word "peace" all too easily obscures the awareness that laying down arms does not simultaneously—and certainly not necessarily—go hand in hand with harmony. Of course, all the Member

States concerned continue to pursue their respective national interests—in particular because in each nation state alone is where the voters responsible for the politicians' re-election live. But even beyond this short-term calculation it is immediately obvious that signing a treaty would not mean throwing overboard the baggage of experience from previous centuries. In the struggle to assert one's own interests, one renounces the use of weapons, but not the attainment of this goal by other means. That is why arduous and seemingly never-ending debates about results that cannot really be predicted *ex ante* are repeated in each case. Such debates are an expression of European diversity and, at least in retrospect, evidence of the uniqueness of the European project.

On the other hand, with regard to the dependence on outlook and experience, the narrative suffers paradoxically from the resounding success that accompanies it. For the first time in European history, the blessing of 70 years of peace has enabled entire generations to grow up for whom armed conflict is at most a matter of foreign news or computer games rather than a matter of personal experience. We don't need to cite behavioral economists' "recency effect," according to which the most recent event has a much stronger impact on consciousness than earlier ones (with the possible exception of the first event, in the so-called "primacy effect"). Simple common sense makes it immediately obvious that for these generations the preservation (not the creation) of peace is not a task that requires constant effort but rather is the natural state of affairs. For these generations, the peace narrative of the European Treaties may not be much more than a nostalgic romanticization of dangers long since overcome.

Since De Gaulle's appeal to the fatherlands (see above), not only the economic but also the political ambitions of the European Union have increased dramatically, the membership has grown enormously (including states that have a completely different historical background and wealth of experience or ballast to offer), and the sphere of influence of "Europe" and its impact, felt directly by each individual, has grown disproportionately compared to the original historical situation. Adding this to our previous analysis, it becomes clear that in this respect too, the peace narrative seems almost like a piece of clothing that has become too tight. Its message no longer does justice to the aspirations and ambitions of the entity. Nothing expresses this state of affairs as clearly as Brexit: Europe's bellicose history has been superseded by the successful history of the Commonwealth. Indeed, the danger remains that other Member States may believe that they can ignore the peace-making power of the Treaties and think that they can achieve their wellbeing along purely national lines.

3. COVID-19 SUGGESTS A NEW SOLUTION

From the circumstances outlined above, we can see that a new narrative is the least that the European idea needs in order to carry on existing. At a time when the search for meaning is increasingly on the agenda, it should be clear that this must not be limited to a purely economic goal. Rather, it must offer a meaning that goes beyond material considerations and is also future-oriented in order to protect it from all too rapid obsolescence. A hint towards such a narrative can be found in the current COVID-19 pandemic—it lies in a commonality of rights and responsibilities.

In order to be able to recognize the suitability of this as a new narrative, we must first take a look to the past. A commonality of rights and responsibilities suggests helping and supporting each another, standing up for one another. In the last millennium-and-a-half of European history, this has happened at best with a view to the interests of individual states ("my enemy's enemy is my friend") but not for the sake of a common goal. As banal as it may sound, the consequence of this deficiency which has gone on for centuries is that such a sense of commonality must be learned in order for it to penetrate the collective consciousness.

For the present author, this necessity can be seen particularly well through a comparison with the history of insolvency law. Even if this may seem far-fetched at first glance, a second, somewhat more focused look shows that the European idea has always been subject to considerable burdens and therefore needs support when it comes to battles concerning the distribution of resources, that is—as in the case of every bankruptcy or insolvency—when a so-called "common pool" problem exists, i.e. if the pot does not contain enough funds to meet all requirements. The most urgent but also the most dramatic example is the Greek crisis and the raging battle for distribution and compensation. As we know, this crisis and the way it was dealt with destroyed a great deal of confidence in Europe, far beyond the most directly affected country of Greece itself.

As with the Greek crisis (at least subliminally), bankruptcies were always about debt/guilt [Schuld], in the Western understanding of the term. Because that was the case, in early Republican Rome the defaulting debtor might be cut to pieces by his creditors (Law of the Twelve

Tables, 450 BCE, along with its echo in Shylock's "pound of flesh" in Shakespeare's *Merchant of Venice*). Equally, from the Middle Ages until well into the modern era, the bankrupt was occasionally threatened with the death penalty, which he tried to evade either by fleeing or by suicide (cf. the Hamburg merchant Bendix Grünlich in Thomas Mann's *Buddenbrooks*). But even if he was allowed to live, the bankrupt was usually condemned to a miserable life, for example in debtors' prison. The fact that this cultural attribution of debt/guilt[3] is by no means natural can be seen in the Eastern Mediterranean of antiquity, where, for example in the Old Testament or in the Code of Hammurabi, debt bondage ended automatically after a few years. Execution was not even an option.

We are gradually approaching this Eastern attitude today. Instead of killing the debtor or at least treating him with shame and disgrace, the law now provides that the creditors can help him get back on his economic feet by bailing out his business. Importantly, due to changes in living and economic circumstances, this 180-degree reversal of creditors' behavior is not an expression of humanity imposed upon them, but an absolutely inevitable consequence of the creditors' own innate interests.[4] And yet the traditional understanding of insolvency law as a law that is at least somewhat punitive is powerful enough to encounter vehement resistance even decades after the bailout option was introduced. Here, too, we have to learn, laboriously and time-consumingly, what is good for us.

In insolvency law this is surprising, as there were occasionally echoes of a rejection of overly rigid accusations and punishments in the West too. For example, if the debtor went bankrupt because he suffered a fateful blow against which he could not with the best will arm himself—a flood, for example, a lightning strike or a major fire—more lenient rules at least were employed. In Germany, the same pattern has been applied repeatedly over the last two decades: if a storm led to the flooding of entire regions (for example, in Saxony or Bavaria), the law was quickly changed to lessen its severity. This is an expression of a commonality of rights and responsibilities, because in this case the old patterns of behavior are inappropriate and run counter to one's own interests.

This brings us back to the current COVID-19 pandemic. In this instance, too, a harmful event is taking place that cannot be attributed to any culpable cause. Like a tsunami, it has wreaked havoc, and it was more or less left to chance whether this tsunami affected someone to their credit or debt. This has also resulted in a "common pool" problem. Here, too, national legislators (virtually worldwide) have intervened immediately to alleviate the worst upheavals.[5]

But here's something completely new: even at the European level, in view of the enormity, the extent, and the seriousness of the crisis, the realization has prevailed that help is needed. And that indeed is what has happened—and to a vast extent. The individual measures include:

1. The European Commission is carrying out a two-tier plan: the first tier aims to strengthen resilience and repair damages—750 billion Euros have been made available for this. The second tier involves a long-term budget of 1.1 trillion Euros.

2. At the same time, the European Central Bank has made available a 750 billion Euro aid package that aims, among other things, to facilitate access to credit.

3. The European Stability Mechanism is offering a two-and-a-half-year-long 240 billion Euro program of particularly cheap loans, with no economic strings attached.

4. The Franco-German proposal of May 18, 2020 is offering a 500 billion Euro rescue package instead of the previously controversial Eurobonds.

It is hard to imagine a more impressive commitment to commonality. It is based not only on altruism, but also and especially on the well-understood self-interests of each Member State—indeed, it is about asserting collective strength. If it were possible to represent and understand this package of measures as the prelude to a new understanding of togetherness, and if the associated narrative were entwined with this idea of collective rights and responsibilities, this would create the foundations on which both current and future generations can acquire an image of Europe that is attractive and promising for the future. It is the creation of a Europe that is certainly always difficult in all its diversity, but a Europe that is always based on commonality and is therefore a place worth living in.

Notes

1. See Christoph G. Paulus, "On the Value of Europe's Diversity" in Corinne Michaela Flick (ed.), *The Standing of Europe in the New Imperial World Order* (Munich: Convoco, 2020), pp. 311–325.

2. This is a reference to the famous witticism in Carol Reed's movie, *The Third Man*. It comes from a monologue, improvised by Orson Welles during filming, that became known in movie history as the "cuckoo clock speech." It was delivered by Harry Lime on the Ferris wheel in Vienna's Prater park. He says: "In Italy for thirty years under the Borgias they had warfare, terror, murder, bloodshed but they produced Michelangelo, Leonardo da Vinci, and the Renaissance. In Switzerland they had brotherly love, five hundred years of democracy and peace, and what did that produce? The cuckoo clock." The sense is that war and terror bring forth great things while peace and democracy only create banal stuff like the cuckoo clock. Later in an interview, Welles explained: "When the picture came out, the Swiss very nicely pointed out to me that they've never made any cuckoo clocks—they all came from the Black Forest..."

3. See Ruth Benedict, *The Chrysanthemum and the Sword – Patterns of Japanese Culture* (Boston, MA: Houghton Mifflin Harcourt, 1946).

4. Cf. Christoph G. Paulus, "Ausdifferenzierungen im Restrukturierungs- und Insolvenzrecht zum Schutz der Gläubiger" in *Juristenzeitung* (2019), p. 11 ff.

5. According to International Monetary Fund estimates (September 2020), more than 11.7 billion dollars have been used to bail out national economies. International Monetary Fund, *Fiscal Monitor: Policies for Recovery* (October 2020), p. xi.

CHAPTER 12

A NEW ALLIANCE OF DEMOCRACIES

SVEN SIMON

In spring 2019, the European Commission published a
strategy paper on the future of EU–Chinese relations.
It stated: "China is, simultaneously, in different policy
areas, a cooperation partner with whom the EU has
closely aligned objectives, a negotiating partner with
whom the EU needs to find a balance of interests, an
economic competitor in the pursuit of technological
leadership, and a systemic rival promoting alternative
models of governance." The Commission thus characterized the People's Republic of China as an "economic
competitor" and as a "systemic rival."[1] This second
characterization in particular represents a decisive

turning point in European foreign policy. As one of the last policy documents published by the outgoing Juncker Commission, it represents a paradigm shift in European rhetoric, the end of an era that the French historian François Godement described as the "honeymoon" of Sino-European relations.[2] According to Godement, said era began in the late 1990s, when the West's outrage over the crackdown on the Tiananmen Square democracy movement gradually subsided and China seemed to be embarking on a new phase of reform and openness, with China joining the World Trade Organization in 2001. However, hopes for China's liberalization were not fulfilled in the years that followed, especially under the aegis of Xi Jinping as paramount leader. Both empirically and anecdotally, we can see that public opinion in the West has become noticeably more skeptical about China and its state system in recent years. Awareness of a shift in the balance between challenges and opportunities created by China has grown in Europe.

Dealing with the resurgence of China not only poses a challenge to individual states, but also sparks new systemic competition between liberal democracies and authoritarian one-party states. Neologisms such as "systemic rivals" evoke associations with the Cold War and of confrontation akin to that with the

Soviet Union. However, unlike the USSR, the Chinese state model under the somewhat cumbersome title of "socialism for the 21st century with Chinese characteristics" is not being exported to other countries. Unlike Moscow, Beijing has not founded its own Socialist International to which parties in other states can belong, and which pursues its own foreign policy interests. Both the supply and the demand for "Xi-ism" as a coherent ideology of state loyalty analogous to the Marxist–Leninist revolutionary exports of the 20th century remain limited outside of China. Against this backdrop, what does it mean to regard the People's Republic as a "systemic rival"?

China uses its own multilateral tools to internationalize its norms. According to Ian Manners (2002), norms can be understood not merely as legal ones that lead to the understanding of practices as "normal," but also as the entirety of all state actions.[3] The transmission belt for this construction of normality includes, firstly, the establishment of one's own international organizations and, secondly, bilateral agreements. This includes institutions such as the Asia Infrastructure Investment Bank (AIIB), the Shanghai Cooperation Organization, and bilateral initiatives under the umbrella of the Belt and Road Initiative. Whilst such mechanisms for exporting norms are surely more diffuse than during previous systemic competitions, they effectively exist in reality. The European Commission describes them in the abovementioned strategy paper as follows:

> China's business and investment activity in third countries, including in the Western Balkans, the EU's neighborhood and Africa has become widespread. Chinese investments have contributed to the growth of many receiving economies. At the same time, these investments frequently neglect socioeconomic and financial sustainability and may result in high-level indebtedness and transfer of control over strategic assets and resources. This compromises efforts to promote good social and economic governance and, most fundamentally, the rule of law and human rights.[4]

In short, the Commission fears that Chinese influence in the indicated regions could potentially undermine Western norms.

BEIJING'S INVESTMENTS IN NORMATIVE INFLUENCE

China's involvement in Central and Eastern European countries, especially in the Western Balkans, offers an interesting case study in this regard. After the 2009 financial crisis, Chinese state-owned companies increasingly sought market access in Eastern Europe.[5] In 2012, the Chinese government set up a credit line of 10 billion US dollars to promote the development of bilateral projects with Central and Eastern European countries. At the same time, a multilateral forum was created, which has become known to the European public as the "16+1 Initiative." This initiative encompasses eleven Eastern and Central European EU Member States (Bulgaria, Croatia, Czech Republic, Estonia, Hungary, Latvia, Lithuania, Poland, Romania, Slovakia, and Slovenia) as well as the five Western Balkan countries recognized by the People's Republic of China (Albania, Bosnia-Herzegovina, North Macedonia, Montenegro, and Serbia). Greece joined in early 2019, prompting a change of name to "17+1."

At the annual meetings of the 17+1, contracts are signed between Chinese companies, most of which are state-owned, and European governments. This leads to investment in infrastructure and energy projects, and corporate acquisitions. The flagship projects include the construction of a motorway between Belgrade and Bar in Montenegro on the Adriatic coast, the high-speed Budapest-to-Belgrade railroad, and investments in Serbian steelworks and iron-ore mines. Such investments are usually financed by the recipient countries through loans from Chinese state banks and linked to certain contractual guarantees.[6]

China's participation in infrastructure projects correlates with direct or indirect violations of European law. According to European law, all state infrastructure contracts above a *de minimis* threshold of 5.3 million Euros must be awarded via an EU-wide tendering process. Member States are expressly prohibited from issuing contracts using individual case laws. In addition, state subsidies of more than 200,000 Euros over a period of three years are considered to be state aid and must be approved by the European Commission.[7] This is intended to prevent the state from selecting champions by intervening in market-based competition and giving them unfair competitive advantages. By contrast, the *modus operandi* of the Chinese approach is fundamentally different. Projects in the 17+1 Initiative are often awarded directly to Chinese state-owned companies, bypassing the public tendering process. In many cases such tenders require *ad hoc* legislation. The national governments of the EU candidate countries in the Western Balkans apparently accept that this will create practical obstacles during EU accession negotiations—which include chapters on procurement and investment law. While European direct investments in the Western Balkans are by nature largely market-oriented, they are state-driven on the Chinese side. Associated with a lack of transparency, such projects are therefore particularly prone to corruption. In addition, there is a lack of checks on financial sustainability, which encourages excess debt. By 2018, Chinese creditors held 40 percent of Montenegro's national debt, 20 percent of North Macedonia's, 14 percent of Bosnia and Herzegovina's, and 12 percent of Serbia's. This development encourages yet more financial dependencies and thus creates opportunities for China to exert political influence. A well-known example of this is when Greece vetoed a resolution in the European Council concerning the human rights situation in China in 2017—very soon after an investment decision by the state-owned Chinese shipping company COSCO benefiting the port of Piraeus had been agreed.

Unlike the EU, China does not make its investments dependent on domestic policy reforms in the recipient countries. This ostentatious lack of interference in domestic affairs, which the state authorities in Beijing take pleasure in announcing while at the same time demanding allegiances in terms of foreign policy, threatens the European integration model in the EU's neighborhood. It creates false incentives for local actors to postpone their own reforms and at the same time to use China as an alternative and supposedly uncon-ditional source of funding to the EU. China is thereby weakening the EU's capacity to involve its neighbor-hood politically in the European integration processes and to export its norms. The European Commission recognizes that such normative conflicts are not neces-sarily the Chinese government's intention: "Very often this practice is not actively pursued locally, but ends up being promoted through sheer inertia, as it reflects China's own corporate behavior and political govern-ance standards."[8] China's normative influence is thus rooted in what at the beginning of the 20th century the Austrian lawyer Georg Jellinek once called the "norma-tive power of the factual." The mere presence of China in trade policy is enough to challenge European efforts to export its own system of norms, even in its immediate neighborhood. Today's systemic competition should be understood under this premise.

MULTILATERALISM AS THE BASIS OF A NEW CHINA POLICY

In practice, Central and Eastern Europe is only a periph-eral region in China's geo-economic and geopolitical activity. Normative conflicts are emerging increasingly with regard to the maritime border and freedom of navigation in the South China Sea, over the status of Hong Kong under the Sino-British Joint Declaration of 1984, and over a variety of trade policy issues. From the European perspective, the focus here is on unfair trading practices. The protection of European companies' intellectual property still falls short: for example, according to estimates by the European Commission, 80 percent of all counterfeit products on the European market come from China. The Chinese judiciary often continues to protect local political interests over the legal claims of foreign investors. The joint venture requirement still widely in existence exacerbates the problem of technology transfer as well as strategic investment in top European technologies—the acquisition of the German robot manufacturer Kuka is one example. In addition, gross distortions of free-market competition sometimes occur as a result of state intervention. One example of this is the exclusion of Western technology companies from almost all digital markets, but also the widespread state practice of selecting so-called champions and undercutting international competition through subsidies. In short, in some cases there is no regulatory level playing field in the competition between the EU and China.

SVEN SIMON

In light of China's increasing political and economic importance, individual liberal democracies can only survive in the long term through coordinated collective action. The existing Western institutions are too small to do this, or their remits not defined accurately enough. For this purpose, after Brexit the British government proposed to set up an alliance of G7 countries plus South Korea, Australia, and India, while D-10 (ten democracies), a strategy forum of the transatlantic think-tank Atlantic Council, has been in existence since 2014. Such a strategic alliance could be the first step towards a more effective multilateral response to China's resurgence as a great power.

In this context, it is important for individual Western actors to resist the temptation to take unilateral action. Any hopes for situational economic advantages through *ad hoc* agreements with Beijing are short-sighted. The example of the uncoordinated negotiations of the US Trump administration, without European, Japanese, and Australian involvement, must serve as a warning in this respect. As a consequence, this US approach increased the willingness of Europeans to quickly conclude their own investment protection agreement with China in order to follow suit in the face of the Phase One Deal. In terms of negotiation tactics, a disciplined transatlantic and Indo-Pacific partnership for dealing with China is likely to be more promising in the long term.

The experiences of the COVID-19 pandemic show the acute need for supply-chain diversification and for Europe to become independent of Chinese producers, not just in medical products. The D-10 could coordinate activities in this respect, as well as in the expansion of critical infrastructures, for example 5G networks. Huawei and ZTE's participation in critical infrastructures in the EU seems negligent given the state influence on the Chinese private sector. Instead, joint trade and technology policy cooperation could lead to the independence of democratic states from Chinese supply chains in critical economic areas. The newly elected US President Joe Biden has already signaled his willingness to do so. With such close coordination on strategic supply chains, our societies could become more resilient and innovative. Such a political decoupling from existing dependencies should, however, be carried out with moderation and under the principle of the primacy of market-economy precepts. Except in clearly defined critical areas, supply chains must be established by the market and not by government intervention.

In trade policy, the D-10 could—possibly with the exception of India, which has traditionally been rather reserved towards trade policy liberalization—provide new impetus for reforming the World Trade Organization. In the medium-long term, one might even consider upgrading existing bilateral trade agreements among the D-10 into a free trade area. This would amalgamate a substantial share of global annual economic output for the foreseeable future, and thus secure the geo-economic position of liberal democracies in their systemic competition with China. Only through such cooperation can the European Union maintain its pioneering role in regulatory issues for the long term, given the decline in its population and economic share. In geopolitical terms, the D-10 could also act as a counterbalance to the increasingly aggressive expansionism of the Xi administration, for example through concerted action against annexations in the South China Sea that breach international law or violations of Hong Kong's autonomy rights. The common attitude towards China should be self-confident and principled, but not hostile or aimed at regime change in Beijing. The latter would maneuver the liberal democracies into a political dead end and, at the same time, create a spiral of escalation in East Asia. Instead, when coming to an agreement, the state leadership in Beijing should be offered the opportunity to save face all the time, and this applies equally to geopolitical and economic issues.

With its expertise in merging different legal cultures into a common internal market, the European Union could be the vital pacemaker of a D-10 alliance. Ultimately, this is also the case because the EU either already has a trade agreement with most of the D-10 countries or is in the process of negotiating one. In short, the European Union must pursue a new multilateral approach in association with other liberal democracies, in order to be able to stay in systemic competition with China over the long term.

Notes

1. European Commission, *EU-China – A Strategic Outlook* (2019), p. 1, https://ec.europa.eu/commission/sites/beta-political/files/communication-eu-china-a-strategic-outlook.pdf (accessed January 18, 2021).

2. François Godement, "China's Relations with Europe" in David Shambaugh (ed.), *China and the World* (Oxford: Oxford University Press, 2020), pp. 251–269, here p. 251.

3. Ian Manners, "Normative Power Europe: A Contradiction in Terms?" in *Journal of Common Market Studies* 2 (2002), pp. 235–258.

4. European Commission, *EU-China – A Strategic Outlook*, p. 4.

5. Ardian Hackaj, "The Pragmatic Engagement of China in the Western Balkans" in *Südosteuropa Mitteilungen* 1 (2019), pp. 66–77, here p. 67, https://cdinstitute.eu/wp-content/uploads/2019/05/Pragmatic-Engagement-of-China-in-the-Western-Balkans.pdf (accessed January 18, 2021).

6. Jacob Mardell, "China's Economic Footprint in the Western Balkans" in Bertelsmann Stiftung (2019), https://www.bertelsmann-stiftung.de/en/our-projects/germany-and-asia/news/asia-policy-brief-chinas-economic-footprint-in-the-western-balkans (accessed January 18, 2021).

7. Regulation (EU) No. 1407/2013.

8. Michal Makocki and Zoran Nechev, "Balkan Corruption: The China Connection" in *European Union Institute for Security Studies* (July 2017) p. 4, https://doi.org/10.2815/53274 (accessed January 18, 2021).

CHAPTER 13

EUROPE SHOULD INTENSIFY ITS COLLABORATION ON DIGITALIZATION

GISBERT RÜHL

The COVID-19 pandemic had a profound impact on Europe. Memories of closed schools, cultural events put on ice, an economy at a standstill, and countless video conferences will remain with us for a very long time. The pandemic has changed many things but has also set a lot in motion, and this was most evident in the area of digitalization. Before the pandemic, while many companies considered "mobile working" merely as Silicon Valley buzzwords and were still operating in technologically obsolete ways, after the COVID-19 outbreak they had to make up ground regarding their digital upgrade sometimes within a few days or weeks. It was a major accomplishment, as many would surely describe it in retrospect. This is also borne out by the figures: in Handelsblatt Satya Nadella, the Microsoft CEO, said that in the third quarter of 2020 Microsoft saw five billion meeting minutes in just one day.[1] That is remarkable—and for me it is once again proof of digitalization's importance to the economy. Companies that promoted digital transformation at an early stage have been able to mitigate the negative effects of the pandemic significantly. Their day-to-day work continues as smoothly as possible—except it takes place at a desk at home.

At Klöckner & Co, one of the world's largest producer-independent distributors of steel and metal products and one of the leading steel service companies, early investment in digitalization has paid off. Like other digital-savvy companies, we mastered the transition to the home office without any problems and at the same time ensured that all employees can continue to work efficiently and productively. At the same time, we have increased the share of turnover via digital channels at a much faster speed to over 40 percent: in this respect the fact that we have been giving digitalization top priority for years is paying off. The digital tools developed by our digital unit, kloeckner.i, are being put to intensive use.

Ultimately, however, it is not just about automating sub-processes using digital tools. We want to create new, platform-based business models through which the core processes at Klöckner & Co can be almost completely automated. Digitalization brings hardly any changes to the structure and organization of a company; rather it supports employees in their daily work using various tools while also integrating customers online. With platform-based business models, employees no longer intervene in the core processes, instead designing the AI-controlled organization through which all core processes work automatically. That is the difference between digitalization and digital transformation.

DIGITALIZATION IS CHANGING THE WORLD OF WORK FUNDAMENTALLY: FROM FLEXIBLE WORKING-TIME MODELS TO THE ELIMINATION OF MANY ACTIVITIES AND A SOCIAL CHALLENGE

Over the next ten years, the world of work will change profoundly through the introduction of digital business models, while digitalization is already having a massive impact on today's world of work. A good sixth of Germany's workforce already enjoys a certain amount of mobile working, whether while traveling or working from home. As a result of the COVID-19 crisis, home office use has multiplied: in 2018, only around 5 percent of the German workforce said that they worked from home on at least half of their working days; in April 2020 it was almost a quarter. Coupled with flexible working-time models such as flexitime and trust-based working, types of freedom are emerging that pay off for employers and employees alike. Today, studies are already showing lower operating costs and higher productivity among employees working from home. In addition, the costs of office space are lower and time is saved commuting between home and work. However, not only the basic conditions, but also the type of work is changing due to the increasing application of digital tools. In Germany, for example, around 5 percent of the voting population now offer their services as so-called "crowdworkers." A range of jobs is emerging in which companies outsource tasks and projects to a group of Internet users via an online platform. The classic relationship between companies and their employees is beginning to disappear, at least to some extent.

Equally, the use of artificial intelligence, or AI for short, opens up numerous opportunities for making tasks and processes simpler, more flexible, and more agile. The increasing use of AI will relieve people of routine activities—but also make jobs superfluous, some of which require very extensive training. I would like to cite two examples. In 2019, for the first time, Google AI achieved a lower error rate in diagnosing lung cancer than very highly trained and experienced radiologists. This brings enormous benefits for patients and the health system, since the treatment of simple cases can be carried out more safely and cheaply than by a specialist. In the first place, doctors are able to save more time that they can apply to more complicated cases. Gradually, however, the AI will become so far advanced that it can even perform more difficult diagnoses, which means that radiologists will have to move into new areas of responsibility in diagnostics or they will become redundant. The other example is the translation industry. Already many pages of documents can be translated within seconds using online AI. Even if the quality of these translations has not yet reached the level of professional translators, the advances made over the past few years are remarkable. It is only a matter of time before human translators are no longer required.

Although this opens up many opportunities, we in Europe and especially in Germany often assume that there will be negative impacts on our society: companies would only maximize their profits using artificial intelligence and automation by employing just a few well-paid employees to automate the core processes. The general public often thinks that in this case a large section of society would no longer be needed and would be paid an unconditional basic income to maintain social stability. But is such a scenario realistic? Even if there were winners and losers in industrial revolutions of the past, over the long term people's quality of life and level of prosperity have increased significantly. Even in the current digital revolution, there is much to suggest that this will happen again. Initially the pioneering companies in their respective industries will achieve excess profits until their competitors have caught up. If competition works well, prices fall due to optimized cost structures, and products and services become affordable for broader sections of the population. Technological progress also creates new products and services—and with them completely new areas of industry with new jobs. In order for these jobs to be created in Europe too, however, we must accept and promote these new technologies and innovations. If we close ourselves off from change, future prosperity will be achieved in other parts of the world. An essential factor in guaranteeing a positive impact on society and on the development of innovations is competition that works well. Politics and competition authorities must ensure that this happens, because the "winner takes all" principle of the platform economy does not create a fair distribution of wealth. The first trends suggesting regulation of the major digital platforms are appearing on the horizon: in the USA some are calling for the break-up of Google; in Europe a legislative proposal to regulate platform companies (Digital Services Act) was announced in December 2020; and Germany is currently working on an amendment to the Act against Restraints of Competition [GWB]. However, due to the exponential development and spread of platforms, we are obliged to act quickly. If it takes years for such regulations to take effect, we will be constantly lagging behind.

IT IS ALMOST IMPOSSIBLE TO CATCH UP WITH CHINESE AND AMERICAN TECHNOLOGY COMPANIES' DOMINANT POSITION IN THE AREA OF DIGITAL PLATFORMS

The dominant business models of the 21st century lie in digital platforms. The world's most valuable and fastest-growing companies use a platform-based business model. Well-known companies such as Amazon, Uber, and Airbnb exemplify this model. Their success clearly demonstrates that their digital services are often more easily accessible and convenient for customers to use than services in the analogue world. There are seven platform companies among the world's top ten companies in terms of market value—ten years ago there was only one. In just a few years, the leading established industrial companies have been replaced by digital challengers such as Apple, Amazon, and Alphabet. And the start-up world is catching up, as most of the so-called "unicorns"—new, unlisted companies with a value of over one billion US dollars—rely on platform-based business models.

The world's most successful platform companies are based exclusively in the United States and China. Microsoft, Apple, and Amazon are each rated higher than all the Dax 30 companies combined. In August 2020, Apple's stock-market value made it the first US company to exceed the $2 trillion mark. In the list of the 20 largest tech businesses, the United States has 12 and China 8 companies—one can search in vain for a European competitor.

What is the reason for the dominant position of American and Chinese tech companies? Businesses in the United States and China are now superior to us

Europeans in many areas. They have huge tech players (originally from the business-to-consumer sector—B2C) who can collect, analyze, and evaluate gigantic amounts of data. In addition, significantly more investment capital is available for technology, innovations, or mergers and acquisitions, and they enjoy a close-knit network encompassing politics, business, and science. Even in the middle of the COVID-19 crisis, companies such as Facebook and Alibaba are investing billions in future technologies, while German and European businesses are pursuing tough austerity measures and halting important investments. Alibaba, for example, is investing 28 billion US dollars in its cloud infrastructure, while companies such as Continental and Daimler are reducing their research spending.

In short, Europe lacks the infrastructure for disruption. This begins with networks and data usage, continues with regulation and financing structures, and culminates in issues such as training, cooperation, and mindset. All these factors are currently preventing disruptive developments and ensuring that other countries can overtake us—and extend their lead. But in Europe the first economic alliances against the overwhelming power of foreign tech companies are emerging. It is questionable, however, whether projects such as the HERE mapping service (an auto-industry alliance against Google) or the so-called Log-in-Allianz, comprising RTL, ProSieben, and Zalando, will stay in business long enough to mature into a long-term relevant player in the field of global digitalization, for although the European Union, with its 446 million inhabitants, has about 118 million more people than the United States, we have structural disadvantages. In Europe we are faced with linguistic, cultural, and regulatory challenges that do not exist in China or the United States. If we consider language alone, this difference becomes particularly clear. In the EU we have 24 different official languages: by comparison 70 percent of Chinese speak Mandarin, and all Americans speak English. One thing is certain, however: European alliances are imperative if we want to maintain our competitiveness, so we have to acknowledge these supposed weaknesses due to structural differences and use the diversity we possess in order to overcome any substantial disadvantage compared with larger individual markets. Indeed, European diversity can be an advantage when it comes to creating innovation. In the development of new approaches in Europe we must collaborate more intensively than large nation states, as we have to mediate between the differences that exist in the individual nation states and their inhabitants in order to achieve our goal. At the same time, by global standards we enjoy significantly more diverse perspectives when we approach a problem collectively. Initially this sounds like two disadvantages, but constructive collaboration and different perspectives are two essential elements in the development of innovations. But these can only prosper with the right fertile ground—appropriate regulations and financial support.

One exciting development can currently be seen in Asia, where billions are being invested in business-to-business platforms (B2B). This might indicate the area where the future of platform-based business models will lie. Traditionally B2B markets are important for Germany in particular, and we see great potential in these markets for our company as well. That is why we founded XOM Materials three years ago, and since then we have come much closer to our goal of building a leading B2B platform for steel and metal products and other materials. Alongside Klöckner & Co, other German and European companies have also recognized that digital platforms create added value in the B2B sector. Examples of functioning solutions are Siemens Lufthansa Technik and ABB with their respective platforms. These initiatives illustrate how the industrial strength of the German economy can be used to drive the platform economy forward in a significant way. I am confident that based on these ambitions, a competitive ecosystem for B2B platforms can develop in Europe, but only if we invest even more, if politicians set up the regulatory framework correctly, and if every company strengthens the willingness of its employees to support and drive forward change.

EUROPE NEEDS AN INNOVATION-FRIENDLY INFRASTRUCTURE AND A COMMON APPROACH— THIS IS THE ONLY WAY WE CAN REMAIN COMPETITIVE AND SECURE OUR PROSPERITY

When it comes to platforms, we in Europe have already made mistakes and have fallen far behind as a result of ossified structures. If you divide the "game" to win a dominant position in the area of platforms into three periods, as in ice hockey, we can see that we have already lost in the first third, the B2C area. In the second period, too—the cloud platforms—other companies have been able to establish themselves. Therefore, the attempt to establish a competitive European cloud against the overwhelming power of Amazon, Microsoft, and Google using GAIA-X is not very promising. The American cloud-service providers are so far ahead that it will be almost impossible to develop an adequate alternative. Equally, a consortium now comprising 300 companies and institutions does not seem in a position to take on the large platform companies effectively. We are simply too far behind in this respect. While US companies and Alibaba in China have been researching and innovating in this field for years, we Europeans launched GAIA-X onto the market in 2020. We have a particular kind of self-image and are following a European path. That is fine, but we should not be under the illusion that we are creating a global champion that can outstrip the established players in this field. Instead of failing with a similar attempt, as was the case with the idea of a European search engine a few years ago, we should acquire the necessary knowledge through the European solution and then concentrate on using the existing—and almost completely fine-tuned—clouds to build digital business models in the B2B sector and Industry 4.0. If we focus on developing industry-specific platforms and applications using the existing cloud platforms, we have a chance of at least keeping up. For this we need an innovation-friendly infrastructure. This includes, for example, a functioning 5G network infrastructure that enables comprehensive data gathering, as well as consistent and industry-friendly regulation of data storage and usage. We have gotten used to having excessive and academic debates about the "right" data strategy, instead of letting companies get on with it. Above all, this regulatory uncertainty prevents urgently needed investment in important areas. The European idea of pluralism stands in the way of efficient and competitive innovation. In the last economic stimulus package, Germany's Federal Government made around two billion Euros available for research on quantum computers in the period up to 2025. However, we are already lagging behind in competition with the United States and China. Apart from that, it is not expedient for us Germans to try to go it alone. With European partners, we could raise significantly more capital and in this way reduce the gap at least. If we fail to do that, we will lose competitiveness in many areas and endanger our prosperity. In 2019 the EU generated a gross domestic product of around 14 trillion Euros, which is slightly more than in China over the same period. Sufficient capital should therefore be available to promote innovation in a targeted manner in the relevant industries. It is high time to conceive of the EU as an economic entity that competes with other world powers. European champions will not only strengthen Europe as a whole but also the nation states—this is the only way we can maintain our European sovereignty and secure our prosperity.

It seems as if we have understood that. In August 2019 the European Commission put forward the idea of a "European Future Fund". It is intended that this fund for the future be endowed with 100 billion Euros so that European companies can overtake the international technology giants. It's a good idea, but it has thus far remained precisely that—just an idea. What is lacking is the single voice of a united Europe that will help technology companies to think European.

Note

1. Axel Postinett, "Microsofts Cloud wächst weiter – aber die ersten Corona-Folgen sind spürbar" in *Handelsblatt*, July 22, 2020, https://www.handelsblatt.com/technik/it-internet/softwarekonzern-microsofts-cloud-waechst-weiter-aber-die-ersten-corona-folgen-sind-spuerbar/26029566.html?ticket=ST-3459171 (accessed February 9, 2021).

CHAPTER 14

HOW COVID-19 CHALLENGES GLOBAL HEALTH POLICY

IN CONVERSATION WITH
GARRETT WALLACE BROWN

Convoco: Governance in global health has experienced a boost since 2000. How has the global health landscape changed?

Garrett Wallace Brown: The last 20 years have witnessed a massive increase in global health institutions, initiatives, and financing. As one example, in the year 2000, at the G8 Summit in Japan, two major initiatives were launched: the Global Fund to Fight AIDS, Tuberculosis and Malaria (GFATM) as well as the Gavi Alliance, which is also known as the Vaccine Alliance. In the case of the GFATM, it received an initial investment of $10 billion. Between 2000 and 2013, development aid for health tripled with an annual growth rate of over 11 percent. This marked the start of a number of major initiatives. One of the more recent is the Global Financing Facility, which was introduced to improve child and maternal health.

These increases were aligned with new policy directives such as the health targets of the Millennium Development Goals (MDGs) and the subsequent Sustainable Development Goals (SDGs). Within the SDGs we saw unique consensus on the normative goal of Universal Health Coverage (SDG3.8), which included coverage of "financial risk protection, access to quality essential healthcare services and access to safe, effective, quality, and affordable essential medicines and vaccines for all." These new governance policies have together resulted in the proliferation of a huge number of global health institutions. In many ways, unlike other global collective action problems, global health has maintained a fairly consistent level of interest. However, it would be a big stretch to suggest that global health policy, as a whole or holistically, has improved drastically. Nor is it reasonable to suggest that we are managing global health sufficiently. Where there has been success, it has been piecemeal and fragmented, and the COVID-19 crisis has exposed many of the existing cracks in global health policy.

C: You have argued that one reason for the slow progress in global health is a form of institutional gridlock. How so?

GWB: One key principle of gridlock is that in global health governance you simply have more actors to coordinate. Each of these actors has their own agendas and interests. When you have more actors working on a single policy you're going to have larger transaction costs in the process of getting them to agree. In current health diplomacy the biggest problems are transactional delays and policy fragmentation where interests are pursued unilaterally. This creates a situation in which you have a substantial number of global institutions with different funding streams and different approaches to global health.

For example, in 2018 there were 3,401 registered global health institutions. This number does not include national and bilateral institutions (such as DFID or USAID), nor any of the UN-based institutions such as the WHO or UNICEF.

Overall, we probably have about 4,000 actors pursuing various health initiatives, some trying to coordinate at the global level, some not. Having these many organizations creates fragmentation. If we look at COVID-19 as an example, the first question exposing fragmentation relates to who is in charge of monitoring, responding, and setting policy? Where do we go for accountability and effective results? The intuitive response would be the WHO, but they're having difficulty coordinating the various institutions due to poor financing, a lack of cooperation from states, and complex political processes in the World Health Assembly. During the Ebola outbreak, the main effort was led outside the WHO, by Doctors Without Borders, a non-governmental organization with limited resources. You could think "okay, maybe it's at national level where we should look, because most of the work on the ground is being done there." Yet this perpetuates disjointed programs that increase risks. The UK, Sweden, Germany, and the United States, for instance, are following different lockdown strategies, with varying and potentially dangerous consequences.

C: To what extent can we see these institutional problems at play during the COVID-19 pandemic?

GWB: Let's take the International Health Regulations (IHR) as an example. This is a set of international regulations that are supposed to help us track and close off trans-border health emergencies. However, the IHR are hugely underfunded by signatory countries and fewer than 50 percent of the states who signed up to them are compliant. This includes high-income states such as France. They were supposed to become compliant in 2016 and it just did not happen.

In the case of COVID-19, not only were states not compliant, some actually violated the International Health Regulations by not raising the alert early enough or implementing the guidelines. The WHO has no authority to enforce this policy, so even if the WHO knows of a threat, they have no ability other than "naming and shaming" a country. But if that country is the United States or China, how are you going to do that without cutting off your arm in terms of funding? President Trump's policy response to withdraw the United States from the WHO illustrates exactly why the WHO has to moderate its actions in order to keep powerful states on board.

In addition, we had national governments unwilling to take the threat seriously early on. The UK and the United States are perfect examples of two countries that sat back and waited for things to unfold. The one thing Trump probably got right was when he said that if there's a hot spot and a cluster, we must isolate it, restricting travel from China. The fact that there was still international travel from parts of China, despite authorities having closed off cities at a local level, baffles the imagination. That's the first principle of quarantine or lockdown: you do it fast, at the smallest level possible, with the infected population, and you do it well.

Then there is the Pandemic Emergency Fund that was launched by the G7 in Germany in 2015. At that summit the G7 leaders professed that "Ebola had been a wakeup call." In response, the G7 announced a financial facility where up to $500 million was meant to be available to a country when an epidemic is threatening to become a pandemic. Nevertheless, it didn't get the full amount of funding promised, nor has it been utilized in the current crisis, largely because it is set up as a loan mechanism at the World Bank. You have to prequalify. China doesn't qualify for it; neither does India. I don't know what the qualification process would look like as an epidemic was unfolding, but I assume it would be shambolic. One senior official at the World Bank said the whole initiative was "a total embarrassment." Moreover, countries that could qualify for the money are already under incredible national debt. So, why would they take out this extraordinary loan amount when they can't pay off their current loans? Or, why would you take out this loan when you know that financial assistance will come anyway if things threaten to get bad enough for other states? The end result is that this is not a way to devise effective health strategies or deliver health security nationally or globally.

As a means to better coordinate efforts, the G7 launched the Global Health Security Agenda, which was endorsed by the G20. Nevertheless, the agenda remains underfunded and there are very poor coordinating mechanisms. A lot of countries have simply not stepped up to the plate. There was supposed to be joined-up thinking and shared technologies on serious threats like antimicrobial resistance (AMR). Sadly, not enough of that happened, and AMR is a huge global threat. We're talking here about an estimated 300 million deaths by 2050.

COVID-19 exposes the humungous cracks in global health governance. National governments weren't linked up to each other, they were not linked up to any institutions at the global level, and they had no preparedness themselves. They just didn't know what to do.

C: You mentioned that global health policy is getting more politicized. Is that not a problem that exacerbates fragmentation and ineffective institutions?

GWB: Yes, it is getting more politicized, but I think it has to be. The notion that health is not political or that it needs to be depoliticized is probably the biggest nonstarter and fallacy within policy debates. Health is deeply political. Getting a treatment that you need is most likely based on a political decision about that treatment being made available. If we want to save massive numbers of lives tomorrow, we give people clean water and soap. That is not a technologically advanced solution, but a solution often not made available for political reasons or due to political failures. I think that to try to depoliticize health is probably the wrong way of thinking about it.

The right way of thinking about it is how to make those political processes more effective and legitimate and how to get compliance with policies—compliance, for example, with the IHRs that are supposed to help trigger alerts and a call to arms when there's an epidemic that threatens to be a pandemic. We also have financial mechanisms that are supposed to be designed for these situations, and there needs to be political commitments to keep them funded properly.

Yet in the case of COVID-19, China did not raise the alarm soon enough for all sorts of incentivized reasons such as direct foreign investment and not looking weak as a government. This is dangerous behavior, since compliance to rules that provide global public goods is crucial.

Regarding the WHO, even though they had information about COVID-19 in November 2019, and potentially even in October, they were not able to sound the alarm because their hands are tied to some extent. Part of this is due to history. They've been blamed in the past for raising an alarm too soon; in other cases, they called it too late. And they don't know how to handle their political position. Having a WHO afraid to play its role properly and to show leadership deeply undermines any chance for a coherent global system, especially when we're talking about pandemics.

In my view, the way around this is to ask: how do you get political buy-in from someone like China? How do you get institutions to have the effectiveness that is required to address these types of threats? How do you get countries like the United States to back something like this, particularly when their domestic political ideologies don't match up with globalized thinking? This is where politics is actually needed, because those are all political questions that can only be resolved through political processes.

C: Among the many actors in global health are private ones such as the Bill & Melinda Gates Foundation. These have significantly grown in influence over the years. How do you view their influence?

GWB: There are two ways to think about this. The first is to suggest that these new foundations, private and multilateral initiatives, create opportunities for innovation. They come in from outside existing pathway-dependent mechanisms to solve a problem. They tend to be focused on one or two health issues, so they can attack something in a functionalist way. People like Bill and Melinda Gates have certainly underwritten a number of innovations in global health. For example, they supported the invention of low-cost and easy-to-build mosquito traps in Africa, which are an inexpensive way to help control malaria in some areas. There have also been new app technologies, lab research, and advancements in health information systems.

The other way to look at these initiatives is to argue that they add to fragmentation and perpetuate the lack of joined-up thinking in global health. With each new initiative and organization, you create additional overlapping jurisdictions, parallel programs, input from massive egos, and personal pet projects. Often these initiatives are tied to businesses, where there is a belief that a particular product or market capability is transferable to the global health context. For example, since 2000 there has been an extraordinary rise in software or app solutions intended to promote public health. In many cases these are novelty projects or lack contextual specificity, often turning them into technological wonders with limited purchase on the ground. This raises many questions about funding sources, epistemic authority, and the power dynamics involved.

Take, for example, a country like Tanzania where 47.5 percent of the health budget is reliant on external funding. Bill and Melinda Gates are significant global health funders. If they put certain conditions on their aid, a country like Tanzania will likely accept it even if the local authorities know that it undermines local ownership or know that the program is not contextually sensitive enough to be the right fit.

This raises big concerns about power and epistemic authority, but also about sustainability. What happens when the funding ends? If the country is not developing, how realistic is it to assume that the country can pick up the slack? Again, that creates go-nowhere, fragmented policies that have a limited shelf life and suddenly terminate. This does not promote long-term global health, at least not in the way that people like Bill and Melinda Gates say they want it to.

C: What about questions of legitimacy, given the extent to which they can shape the agenda for global health?

GWB: Going back to Bill and Melinda Gates, there's a huge concern about the issue of epistemic authority that I alluded to before. They are knowledge authorities, similar to influential journals. Yet this raises questions about the source of that authority. Why should an individual like Bill Gates have the same vote on the Global Fund board as the EU or the United States? Why should Bill Gates, as a single person, be the second-biggest donor to the WHO after the United States? And with what policy consequences? Why is he on TV telling us that Trump is wrong about cutting funding to the WHO?

There is a worry that money buys you access to policymaking and to setting the agenda. This raises additional questions about accountability and transparency. President Trump is accountable to Congress, to the Supreme Court, to the checks and balances in the US State Department, and ultimately to the US voter. Who is Bill Gates accountable to? There's no constituency. The same goes for transparency. Trump, who made many errors when it comes to COVID-19, was heavily scrutinized by the media. But you don't see that same level of scrutiny for Bill Gates, a man who single-handedly underwrote the Global Fund for almost two years during the financial crisis.

If there's a perception that Bill Gates has little legit-imacy with no accountability and transparency, you will lose buy-in quickly. There will be compliance problems or more dead-end, go-nowhere policies. On the other hand—and this is the innovation argument—if people think he has a lot of legitimacy and is doing good work, then we may welcome this one person taking charge, since he can sidestep the gridlock that exists at the global level.

The question is: do you take a utilitarian approach in the sense that the end justifies the means, or do you take a procedural approach and say "one has to have appropriate procedures because what's good today may not be good tomorrow and one person shouldn't have that much authority?" I favor the latter.

C: Private actors provided much needed funding in recent years, but in the long term these are legitimacy questions that undermine the whole structure of the global health system.

GWB: Yes, absolutely. I think all of us agree the WHO needs serious reform or should be replaced by a different institution. And nobody thinks that the WHO is completely hopeless—although it is getting close to becoming inert. Part of its hopelessness, unfortunately, has been due to ring-fenced funding. Members used to pay their dues and the WHO could spend that money on global policies directed by the World Health Assembly and other programs in the WHO.

Today, only about a third of their budget is free for them to choose how to spend it. The other two-thirds are ring-fenced around national-interest, pet projects, or aligned programs. The WHO can only use that money in certain ways, as specified by the states that give them the money. This adds to fragmentation, an inability to generate economies of scale, and a lack of joined-up, long-term thinking.

C: The approach of nation states to global health is often characterized as one of securitization, focusing on containment and surveillance. Do we need to do more in respect to prevention and strengthening health systems?

GWB: I'm a firm believer that an ounce of prevention is worth a pound of cure. COVID-19 is going to cost us trillions of dollars, but it didn't need to.

It would cost an absolute minuscule fraction of that to get a fit-for-purpose institution at global level and to strengthen health systems in countries where these threats usually originate. It's not a surprise that Ebola started in West Africa with their weakened health systems. Even wealthy countries suffer from a lack of comprehensive and preventative medicine, while ignoring upstream social determinants of health. SARS and now COVID-19 originated in China. This is not a poor health system and they should have been able to respond to this. It shows that the Chinese health system also needs to be more comprehensive than it is. Furthermore, it demonstrates how contextual factors like politics and non-epidemiological economic considerations can greatly influence health outcomes. Culture also plays a huge role. Popular food markets known to foster zoonotic diseases should not be allowed to continue to operate in the way they do. That is a basic sanitation and epidemiological no-brainer that should have been addressed after SARS. In summary, my position is that proper disease control requires strengthened health systems, a rethink of the IHRs, proper monitoring and compliance systems,

quick response to emerging pathogens, and total isolation at the smallest level possible before spread, while
supporting the global common good of public health.
These are small investments when you compare it to
the expenses and costs caused by COVID-19.

C: Do we need a more holistic approach to global
health? Many people don't seem aware of the importance of social and environmental factors, particularly
in the case of infectious diseases.

GWB: Yes, a big problem is what some colleagues and
I have called the Pasteurian paradigm, which suggests
that each pathogen has one cure. You wait for the pathogen to arrive, you go into lockdown, and you wait for
a vaccine to show up. This is the COVID-19 strategy,
yet there is no guarantee that we will always find a
vaccine. The logic of this Pasteurian model suggests
that there is something fundamentally wrong with
the way we are thinking about where pathogens—
viruses—come from. They don't just emerge from a
vacuum; they emerge from certain environmental
and social determinants. Like you said, we often don't
think about the social origins of these pathogens.

Think, for example, about markets that handle
food, how they cohabitate animals that shouldn't be

next to each other, allowing them to cross-pollinate pathogens. Or consider how we destroy ecosystems, causing humans to live in closer proximity to certain animals or insects that are known to carry diseases, such as forest bats and deer ticks. Or consider how our lifestyles enhance the danger of this disease with its mortality rates linked closely to comorbidities. These are all social factors that could be changed, or areas where we could apply preventative measures in a more longitudinal fashion.

My colleagues and I are trying to suggest that this "one pathogen one cure" mentality, and the idea that science will vaccinate us out of problems, reduces long-term preventative thinking. It simply fails to comprehend sufficiently the need for strengthened health systems, thinking about the way we come into contact with certain animals, or reducing the amount of antibiotics we give to our animals unnecessarily, which, when done badly, helps to create antimicrobial resistance. These are social behaviors. If we take those into account more thoroughly, we won't have to rely on always finding a vaccine in a hurry. We need to put existing paradigms in perspective. In the case of HIV/AIDS we still don't have a cure; we just have a way of keeping people alive and it's very expensive to do so.

Many scientists don't like it when you suggest that the Pasteurian paradigm is part of the problem. There is still a very 1950s' view that science will save us—much like a religion. Many of my scientist friends just cannot see beyond narrow disciplinary boundaries, ranking the "hard sciences" as hierarchically better than social approaches and thus undermining many of the suggestions I've made about prevention. For me, the hierarchical distinctions are a fallacy: it is not a zero-sum equation, the approaches are not mutually exclusive. In fact, in this case, they are necessarily co-constituted.

C: You have already said a lot about what can be improved, but in your opinion, what is the most important thing the international community can do to curb the risk of future pandemics?

GWB: Different ideas have been mentioned recently: there has been talk of a European health system, of a G20 for health, and Gordon Brown even suggested a temporary world government for health. The BMJ featured an article with the idea of a vaccine-purchasing agency at the global level to respond to the fact that there are too many actors trying to buy things up, creating shortages, and competitive markets that price people out. I think these are all good, short-term, minor iterative responses, but they're not sufficient. They still look temporary, ad hoc, disjointed, and state-centric.

Instead, some colleagues and I have been floating an idea about what we call world health systems thinking. Health system thinking has been central at the national level for years. It is a holistic approach that covers the six WHO building blocks: service delivery, health workforce, information systems, access to medicines, finance, and governance. These functions must be sufficiently covered by a health system and joined up.

At the moment we are bringing health systems thinking into debates at the global level and would use these six core functions (plus an additional one on populations) as a way of examining and exposing current gaps in the system. There are issues with the building blocks and they are not uncontroversial, so part of this project is to address those issues, as well as make sure that the principle of subsidiarity and local health system strengthening and contextualization are factored appropriately when we scale-up to the global level. A colleague and I are working on this project now and aim to get funding to apply the model, conduct feasibility analysis, and create a series of recommendations. Once we have identified the gaps, we can start thinking about how to fill them: what goals associated with financing, health workforce, information systems, governance, access to medicine, and service delivery would be necessary to fight something like COVID-19.

The approach gives us a toehold on the huge amorphous thing that is how to think about effective global health governance. It provides us with a particular way of looking at it more holistically and an analytical, heuristic tool to get in there. Beyond health systems thinking we have to also start thinking about factors like planetary health, ecological systems, and environmental determinants of human health. Corporations and corporate behavior are also a significant determinant of health.

In other words, we need joined-up thinking that looks at global health as a system, with corresponding functions and delivery mechanisms.

C: This approach would call for more centralization at governance level to escape fragmentation.

GWB: It could be more centralized, or it could be layered with mutual accountability mechanisms. There are all sorts of creative ways you can think about it.

You don't want to just replicate the state at global level; it's not the same animal.

The key is to be reflective and creative. For example, perhaps the WHO building blocks, which we're using for our current model, aren't appropriate and we have to think of something new. The key is to remember what the famous essayist Montaigne said about the idea of change, and I paraphrase: we must start by recognizing that what we are currently doing is bad, and that we would like it to be better.

Unfortunately, my guess is that the international community will only fix the pandemic monitoring system and that some individual states will create emergency stockpiles and rethink their own internal policies. This will be better, but still insufficient. It will be done on the cheap with market solutions where possible to finance it. Why? Because that's how it is always done.

However, half-solutions will not alleviate long-term problems. As we reach 10 billion people on this planet, the number of epidemics turning into pandemics is going to increase. Nature has a wonderful knack of figuring out ways around every counter-measure we can think of. So we need those measures to be as strong as possible. It is just a matter of time before these viruses will mutate and adapt. They don't care about borders, they don't care about egos, they don't care about money, they don't care about political power. These pathogens are singular in their design—they just want to replicate and they need hosts to do so.

C: Any major overhaul of the global health system will require a lot of political will. For example, the idea of a European health system that you briefly mentioned has long been discussed but never seriously approached, partly because it appeared too difficult to get citizens on board. Do you think global health crises like the one we are experiencing will help citizens to recognize the world as a global community, increasing our concern for the health of those abroad?

GWB: My immediate answer is no. COVID-19 will not build solidarity in some sort of metaphysical way, in the sense that we accept some kind of moral obligation to other human beings based on our humanity alone. That said, I believe that COVID-19 could build mutual self-interest. With time, and if properly harnessed, this mutual recognition of interest may underwrite greater sentimentalities towards others, which could form a basis of solidarity.

Basically, the process would be that through our own self-interest we recognize that others have mutual self-interests and that a collective action problem like COVID-19 cannot be solved by one single country, one individual, or even a group of individuals or states. Thus COVID-19 may increase our conception of shared goals and common interests and lead to an emergence of solidarity. Whether or not that means we're going to see others as citizens of the world in a metaphysical sense, in the kind of way that cosmopolitans like Immanuel Kant or the Stoics wanted us to, I doubt that will happen anytime soon.

Yet COVID-19 and its physical and social impacts might be enough to spark greater global cooperation at a functional and practical level, in turn seeing each other as being more in a relationship of solidarity that will strengthen greater identification with each other as global cohabitants. Now this form of solidarity-building happened at the state level many years ago, when people started to recognize that they shared mutual self-interests, which then called for a super-state or some sort of institutional binding agent to secure those mutual interests. History is full of empirical examples of communities coming together to form wider societies. Therefore, I don't think it is impossible to think about these processes taking place at the global level.

The personal and communal motivation offered by COVID-19 toward a larger world-view is driven by what is often called a world risk society. This is an idea by the late German sociologist Ulrich Beck. Beck argued that large human existential threats like COVID-19 create a common understanding of collective risk and that this collective risk can underwrite social change towards common or cosmopolitan identities. He was a historical sociologist and looked at history to try to bear this out convincingly. His best example relates to the fact that you would have no UN without World War II and the Holocaust. It took a world risk society generated by the prospect of total war to get that kind of global solidarity. And many of the international laws we know today, such as the Geneva Convention, would not have emerged without those terrible human tragedies.

In his writings, Beck speculated that climate change was the next risk catalyst that would bring us to a world risk society and create cosmopolitan identities. But I think that is wrong: climate change is too slow-burning and not immediate enough. It's just not at the same level of consciousness as COVID-19, which has affected everyone and is estimated to have half the world's population in lockdown.

In other words, COVID-19 and its risks, real or constructed, is palpable, it is experienced, it is immediate, and we all understand the costs—the cost to our social lives, cost to our wellbeing, cost to our jobs, cost to our economic security, from mass unemployment to the rise of domestic violence. The crisis is now, not tomorrow, and we are experiencing it in real time. I think this lived immediacy is a really important psychological driver for a shift from self-interest to mutual-interest, to new sentimentalities, to understanding a shared history, to emerging values, to solidarity and collective action. If any event has a chance to create a world risk society with a future of more solidarity, then this would be it. This crisis has the potential to help us to rethink our paradigm.

As Hegel says, "the Owl of Minerva only spreads its wings with the coming of the dusk," the idea being that knowledge is only found when the day has ended and you can look back on it reflectively. Most people read Hegel's statement negatively, but I think that the horizon is upon us now and Minerva, being a symbol of knowledge, has the opportunity to spread its wings, not because it is the end of the day, but because there is a transition to the beginning of the next. Let's hope that we all reflect on the coming darkness properly.

CHAPTER 15

COVID-19 AND THE ROBERT KOCH INSTITUTE: THE FRAMEWORK AND ESSENTIAL CONSIDERATIONS FOR COMBATING A PANDEMIC IN GERMANY

LOTHAR H. WIELER

SUMMARY

The current COVID-19 pandemic clearly shows that a pandemic can go far beyond a mere health crisis, as it has additional, far-reaching economic, ecological, and socio-political consequences. The current international health crisis also proves that the warnings of many scientists and those in positions of responsibility about the consequences of this pandemic caused by a highly contagious pathogen were justified. Equally we can say that many countries are not adequately prepared for pandemics and that the weakest link in the chain determines the success of the other countries.[1] These facts—together with the prediction that this will not have been the last pandemic—require all countries to have both a clear strategy for combating the current pandemic and strategic, sustainable preparations for future pandemics. It goes without saying that an adequately equipped health system is necessary for the success of such a campaign. But unfortunately, not everyone is aware that this primarily affects public health capacity, in addition to outpatient and inpatient healthcare. This includes the public health service, without which it is impossible to contain a pandemic. Accordingly, the public health sector must at last be given the attention and appreciation it deserves through adequate support in terms of staffing and finance. Furthermore, good governance and an educated and resilient population are an essential foundation for combating pandemics successfully. It is therefore important in future to involve the population in national research agendas both through various interest groups and in transdisciplinary research projects. Indeed, due to the severe impact of pandemics on society as a whole, an interdisciplinary approach in science alone is not enough.

INTRODUCTION

This essay offers an overview of the legal, institutional, and professional framework as well as strategies for coping with a pandemic in Germany, but it does not describe the strategy for combating it in detail. We must emphasize explicitly that without an appropriate level of education and empowerment among the population as well as good governance by the respective state leaderships, even a good professional and institutional foundation is no guarantee that the crisis can be combated adequately. Without confidence in the agents involved, a pandemic can only be contained to a limited extent. Alongside professional expertise and sufficient resources, one basis for such confidence is states' research agendas in which, beyond the integration of various disciplines (i.e. interdisciplinarity, the combination of different scientific disciplines), a kind of transdisciplinarity is practiced, namely the additional involvement of interest groups (stakeholders) in the respective research processes.

Transdisciplinarity is a *conditio sine qua non*, especially for success in sustainability and resilience research.[2] Therefore, in addition to professional, infrastructural, and financial resources, transdisciplinarity forms the crucial basis for dealing with such a dramatic event in society. In Germany, this approach in the area of infection research is currently only implemented conceptually by the research consortium InfectControl2020.[3] The Future Forum Public Health,[4] which was founded a few years ago on the initiative of the Robert Koch Institute (RKI), among others, also aspires to transdisciplinarity. This essay does not deal with the influence of fake news and conspiracy theories, nor with the problem of infodemics, i.e. a flood of false information. But one thing is clear: these elements have a major impact on the success of pandemic containment.

What are the recipes for success in optimal pandemic control? As a priority, there is a clear strategy, the aim of which is to protect the health and lives of as many people as possible. This strategy is included in the influenza pandemic plan, which also forms the basis for combating the COVID-19 pandemic.[5] This plan is based on three cornerstones: containment, protection, and mitigation. However, these three cornerstones not only have to be tackled by the three departments in the health system (public health service, outpatient care, and inpatient care), but equally society as a whole must make an effort and show solidarity. In this context, the "whole-of-government" approach is applied at government level.[6] Since a pandemic affects many areas of society, the coordinated cooperation of various ministries, public administrations, and public institutions is required, because the only way to combat the pandemic is to work together. These relationships are clearly described in the document "Rahmenkonzept mit Hinweisen für medizinisches Fachpersonal und den Öffentlichen Gesundheitsdienst in Deutschland" [Framework with guidance for medical professionals and the public health service in Germany].[7]

THE FRAMEWORK FOR COMBATING PANDEMICS

Just what is a pandemic? It is defined as an epidemic "occurring worldwide or over a very wide area, crossing international borders and usually affecting a large number of people".[8] So the crucial thing about managing a pandemic is not just the resilience of a national health system and its local authorities, but also the international communication channels and supranationally developed strategies for action, such as the plan for the risk management of a global influenza pandemic which has been developed and continuously updated by the WHO since the 1990s.[9] The central global framework agreement for the prevention and management of epidemics are the International Health Regulations (IHR),[10] the current version of which was ratified in 2005 by the WHO's annual World Health Assembly (WHA). This means that there exists a clear framework for national preparations, including plans to tackle pandemics.

The dynamics whereby infectious diseases spread as a result of population growth, urbanization, aging, migration, international trade and travel connections, air traffic, and the adaptation of microorganisms are increasing globally.[11] Recent outbreaks such as SARS in 2003, influenza in 2009, E. coli in 2011, MERS-CoV in 2012, and Ebola in 2014/15 show the differing degrees of resilience in health systems that operate on the basis of prevention and preparedness, i.e. the extent to which people, resources and interventions are prepared and ready to go. The "silent" pandemic of antibiotic-resistant bacterial pathogens should not go unmentioned in this context, as it is usually only highlighted in the event of acute outbreaks, but in fact represents an enormous and continuously increasing burden of disease.[12]

Over the last few decades we have seen again and again that the fight against epidemics was focused initially on purely biomedical interventions, although the implementation of interventions can only succeed if those affected, i.e. the population of the relevant country or region, understand and accept them. Therefore, the social and behavioral sciences in particular must also be involved. Another important aspect is the immense challenge of risk communication. These disciplines should therefore be intensively promoted and enhanced as well, because a pandemic can only be controlled if it is possible to plausibly justify and communicate protective measures within the overall social context.

A note on the German health system: the two cornerstones of outpatient care and inpatient care are receiving sufficient attention. They are very well equipped and now have an annual turnover of well over 300 billion Euros in Germany. By contrast, the third cornerstone, the public health service, received little attention before the COVID-19 pandemic, both in terms of media coverage and in professional medical circles. However, the fundamental importance of the public health service, whose expertise comprises many more elements than just protection against infection, is coming under intense scrutiny in the context of the current COVID-19 pandemic. Without the generic measures of protection against infection—prevention through self-protection, hygiene, quarantine, and isolation—Germany would be faring significantly worse in the COVID-19 pandemic, with the population currently lacking immunity to SARS-CoV-2 and an absence of vaccines and specialist therapies in the run-up to Christmas 2020. Contact-tracing, quarantine (segregation of those suspected of being contagious), and isolation (segregation of those infected and sick) are the universal basis for combating epidemics, because those who are infected or are suspected of being contagious, who are also not in contact with other people, pose no risk of infection to others when in quarantine or isolation. It is only thanks to these tools that future outbreaks can be suppressed efficiently; alongside the responsible behavior of our fellow citizens in this pandemic caused by a respiratory pathogen (maintaining a safe distance, observing hygiene rules, wearing a mask) they form the basis of success.

Experiences of crisis continue to reveal the crucial significance of monitoring and make clear the importance of digital applications.[13] This includes setting threshold levels for outbreak signals and evaluating signals, as well as carrying out a standardized risk assessment on a low-threshold basis. This is a continuous assessment of the situation in the classic sense, and the more well-founded it is, the more precisely the decisive indicators can be assessed. If an epidemiological situation has emerged, crisis structures are activated, tasks are prioritized, and risk assessments are carried out repetitively to deal with it. Recommendations must be drawn up on the basis of evidence identified and generated, which are then communicated to specific target groups; measures to protect against infection must be adapted if necessary and implemented, and the safeguarding of medical care monitored.

The assessment of a pandemic situation by means of surveillance comprises three areas. First, the dynamic of the infections: in this instance we usually use the number of reported cases to record and calculate incidences. In the current pandemic, for example, the 7-day incidence of 50/100,000 has established itself as the threshold level that is used worldwide. Furthermore, the course of the infection is characterized, for example, by the effective R-number, an estimate of how many people on average are infected by one infected person. This number fluctuates greatly depending on the biological properties of the pathogen (contagiousness, infectiousness), but it also depends on people's behavior: during the current COVID-19 pandemic, the focus is on transmission via exhaled droplets and aerosols. Therefore, gatherings in close proximity over longer periods of time are an ideal way for SARS-CoV-2 to be transmitted by infected people to others. This epidemiological data can be related separately to individual geographical areas, areas of life, and certain groups of people, depending on the kind of information collected while safeguarding data protection and practicability. The data is of huge importance because it allows us to compare different countries and regions worldwide, given consistent case definitions. Diagnostic testing should also be included. In this instance, the testing strategy of each geographical region plays a role and of course, depending on this testing strategy, the positivity rates as well. For example, the WHO estimates a threshold value of 5 percent positivity rate as the point when individual countries could normalize public life again, provided that this value has not been reached for at least two weeks. From all the above-mentioned information we can derive guidelines as to whether, for example, infections are occurring in the form of outbreaks or whether there is so-called community transmission, i.e., a spread of infection that can no longer be traced.

The second essential aspect is the severity of the illness. The manifestation index (the number of those infected who become ill) and the severity of the disease, the long-term consequences of the infections and mortality are all important indicators. It is also important to identify those groups in the population who are at particular risk of developing a severe form of the disease.[14] The severity of the disease can only be properly identified at the start of a pandemic if the country in question has established a system of meaningful surveillance. In Germany, this has been possible because the Robert Koch Institute—in addition to the statutory official reports of case numbers including a variety of metadata on individual cases—has over the years established various tools for syndromic surveillance, with which the severity of respiratory infections, in particular critical cases of pneumonia, can be analyzed in real time. This has been done on the one hand via a citizen science project (GrippeWeb) and on the other hand via ICOSARI, a survey that records cases of severe pneumonia in hospitals. In addition, the Working Group on Influenza is analyzing the occurrence and typology of viral respiratory pathogens as part of a sentinel system. All the surveillance tools are summarized on the RKI website and in a recent article.[15] Additional tools were set up in the context of the COVID-19 pandemic.[16]

The third area is the capacity of the above-mentioned three cornerstones of the health system. If one of the areas is overburdened, the pandemic can no longer be fully controlled. Once the health authorities can no longer trace entire chains of infection, new outbreaks will occur, and in the case of the COVID-19 pandemic, as the lungs are a manifestation organ, the system's capacity for ventilation in particular represents an important variable.[17] It is important to note, however, that the vast majority of COVID-19 patients are treated in the outpatient or inpatient departments and not in intensive care units, which is why focusing on the intensive care units does not reveal the whole picture.

As already mentioned, a summary of the corresponding activities can be found in a framework document that was developed under the auspices of the RKI.[18]

The course of an epidemic or pandemic can be divided into four phases. These cannot be strictly separated from one another, since the situation can develop in a highly dynamic way and transitions are fluid. Interventions are implemented according to each particular situation and differ in terms of the point of application, the chosen strategy, and the intended goal. Initially, the focus is on containing outbreaks and protecting vulnerable groups, and this focus will remain central throughout the entire course of the pandemic. If the infection persists, interventions are introduced to mitigate the consequences, which are intended to avoid a serious progression of the disease and overburdening of the healthcare systems. In the recovery phase, regulations can be relaxed or lifted according to the situation. The results of an evaluation of the entire course of the infection are fed back into the process to prevent and prepare for future outbreaks.[19]

Good cooperation between different political levels from the local to the highest is also crucial for combating infectious diseases effectively. In Germany, the legal underpinning is provided by the Act on Prevention and Control of Infectious Diseases in Humans (Infection Protection Act; IfSG[20]), the Administrative Act for IfSG Coordination, the International Health Regulations (IHR[21]) and the IHR Implementation Act (IGVDG[22]). If a disaster is declared, the basis is provided by the Basic Law with its Articles concerning states of tension and national defense as well as legal and administrative assistance in the event of a disaster, and the Civil Protection and Disaster Relief Response Act.

In the event of supraregional outbreaks in Germany, the Robert Koch Institute as the central research and reference facility for infectious diseases in humans in the Federal Ministry of Health is responsible for assessing the situation, for information processing, as well as for communications, analyzing interventions, and diagnostic procedures. The RKI's responsibilities in the area of infectious diseases are structured in more detail in the IfSG. In this case, the RKI is assigned the role of a central federal institution; the IGVDG is also relevant in this context. After September 11, 2001 and the anthrax attacks in the United States, prevention, detection, and damage limitation in the event of aggressions or attacks with biological agents were included within the existing legal framework as a special area of responsibility. Information processing includes the generation, collection, analysis, and evaluation of data, the development of recommendations and—if a request for administrative assistance is made—the on-site investigation of an outbreak. Communications and coordination operate both horizontally and vertically as well as nationally and internationally. In addition to the RKI's high level of scientific expertise, detailed knowledge of the implementation structures and legal framework is of crucial importance in assessing the complexities of data collection and data analysis that arise in the context of a pandemic. In addition, the recommendations must be workable.

The RKI reports data about the epidemiology of the infection to the European authority, the European Center for Disease Control (ECDC), and to the World

Health Organization (WHO). Information is exchanged regularly via the web-based platform EWRS (Early Warning and Response System), which links the ECDC, the EU Commission, EU states, and other states in the European Economic Area in a network. Information is also exchanged between WHO countries using the high-security platform EIS (Event Information Site), which national contacts (National Focal Points) can access in the event of incidents relevant to the IHR. In addition to these official information channels, exchanges are ongoing at national and international level, both bilaterally and multilaterally. These are organized by the WHO or by individual national public health institutes such as the RKI.

To review the structures set up to enforce the IHR, the WHO recommends the voluntary implementation of a so-called Joint External Evaluation (JEE), in addition to mandatory annual self-assessment which evaluates a country's capacities to prevent, identify, and react as quickly as possible to health risks. Germany undertook a JEE for the first time in 2019 and sought advice from the WHO and external experts from other countries. The four main components of the WHO's IHR monitoring and evaluation framework (MEF) are mandatory annual reporting (SPAR), after action reviews (AAR), simulation exercises (SimEx) and the JEE.[23] The framework developed under the leadership of the RKI[24] already contains lessons learned from the JEE.

Another very successful operational structure is the Global Outbreak Alert & Response Network (GOARN),[25] which was founded in 2000, is based at the WHO in Geneva, and supports the fight against disease outbreaks in the form of a network of more than 200 partner countries worldwide. Among other bodies, the US Centers for Disease Control and Prevention, Public Health England, UNICEF, Doctors Without Borders, and the RKI are also involved. In 2019, the RKI was named the world's first WHO Collaborating Center for GOARN.[26] As part of GOARN, employees are sent on overseas missions if requested. Over the past five years, the RKI has been involved in a total of 14 GOARN operations with over 100 missions, five of which taking place as part of the work to contain the COVID-19 pandemic: these were missions to Iran, the Philippines (2x), to Tajikistan and to Turkmenistan (as of November 15, 2020).

In addition, as part of its worldwide cooperation during the COVID-19 pandemic, the RKI has so far supported more than 60 countries with field operations (assessment or training), diagnostics (laboratory equipment, diagnostic material), and technical advice.

This is where the intensive international research of recent years has paid off, research that has once again been supplemented with excellent results through the Global Health Protection Programme (GHPP).[27]

The International Association of National Public Health Institutes (IANPHI) pursues a peer-to-peer approach comparable to that of the JEE in terms of empowerment and capacity-building. This organization, currently comprising more than 100 national public health institutes from over 90 countries, aims to strengthen global capacities in the field of public health.[28] Here, too, the RKI has been involved from the beginning as a founding member.

During an infection, local authorities are an indispensable part of Germany's public health service (ÖGD). A risk assessment for the population is only possible by creating and passing on reports to the higher-level authorities. In addition, health departments have a responsibility to help contain an outbreak through contact-tracing. In combating the current SARS-CoV-2 pandemic, it became clear that it was imperative to strengthen the ÖGD. Short-term solutions in the form of support staff from other authorities as part of an intersectoral health policy ("health through all policies") were welcomed; but even the medical students trained by the RKI remotely as containment scouts or other health professionals offer merely an interim solution. According to a current plan by the federal and state governments a "pact for the public health service" would see four billion Euros of federal government money flow into local authorities' coffers over the next five years, 3.5 billion of which alone is to be used to expand the workforce and increase the appeal of the ÖGD.[29]

In addition to biomedical and epidemiological research for a better understanding and solution of the medical tasks connected with the pandemic, there has also been successful investment in digital solutions in many parts of the healthcare system. For example, within a very short space of time the RKI has developed the Corona Data Donation App, the Corona-Warn-App, and the DIVI intensive care register at national level, working with telecoms providers, start-up companies, and specialist bodies, and has created mobility profiles of the population using aggregated, anonymized cellphone data (as of November 15, 2020). The latter can be used to show the effectiveness of interventions to limit contacts.

CONCLUSION

A pandemic caused by a pathogen that can be transmitted via the respiratory tract and against which the population of the world has no immunity, represents an immense challenge for society as a whole with a corresponding burden of disease. This crisis is not just a health crisis; it also has far-reaching economic, ecological, and socio-political consequences. We must remember that the economy and health are two sides of the same coin, and must not be played off against each other.[30] For Germany, as for many other countries, however, striking a balance between health and economic wellbeing during the SARS-CoV-2 pandemic represents a major challenge.[31] Indeed, it is not yet possible to predict how great a burden COVID-19 will place on society's social and financial security systems by comparison with the diseases that are emerging as a result of the protective measures. Cohort studies with longer follow-up periods will show how restrictions in public life and physical distancing are affecting, for example, mental health or the development of different population groups. The COVID-19 pandemic will only be under control when a significant part of the world population—we are currently assuming around two-thirds—has developed immunity against the virus through vaccination. This point will be reached at different times in different regions of the world. The more solidarity the global community can show in the distribution of vaccines, the sooner adequate immunity can be achieved across individual countries. With both immunity and preparedness, the same principle applies: the weakest link in the chain determines the success of all. Therefore, we should all take care to strengthen every single country. Health equity, health as an equal right for everyone—that should be the goal of us all.

Notes

1. *Global Preparedness Monitoring Board, A World at Risk*, Annual Report, September 2019, https://apps.who.int/gpmb/assets/annual_report/GPMB_annualreport_2019.pdf (accessed January 12, 2021); https://www.ghsindex.org (accessed January 12, 2021); Deutscher Bundestag, *Bericht zur Risikoanalyse im Bevölkerungsschutz* (2012), document 17/12051, January 3, 2013, https://dipbt.bundestag.de/dip21/btd/17/120/1712051.pdf (accessed January 12, 2021).

2. Carolina Adler, Gertrude Hirsch Hadorn, Thomas Breu, Urs Wiesman and Christian Pohl, "Conceptualizing the Transfer of Knowledge across Cases in Transdisciplinary Science" in *Sustainability Science* 13 (2018), pp. 179–190.

3. https://www.infectcontrol.de/de (accessed January 12, 2021).

4. https://zukunftsforum-public-health.de (accessed January 12, 2021).

5. Robert Koch Institute, *Nationaler Pandemieplan Teil I: Strukturen und Maßnahmen*, March 2, 2017, https://www.gmkonline.de/documents/pandemieplan_teil-i_1510042222_1585228735.pdf (accessed January 12, 2021); Robert Koch Institute, *Nationaler Pandemieplan Teil II: Wissenschaftliche Grundlagen*, https://www.rki.de/DE/Content/InfAZ/I/Influenza/Pandemieplanung/Downloads/Pandemieplan_Teil_II_gesamt.pdf?__blob=publicationFile (accessed January 12, 2021).

6. Tom Christensen and Per Lægreid, "The Whole-of-Government Approach to Public Sector Reform" in *Public Administration Review* 67 (2007), pp. 1059–1066.

7. Robert Koch Institute, *Rahmenkonzept mit Hinweisen für medizinisches Fachpersonal und den öffentlichen Gesundheitsdienst in Deutschland*, October 2019, https://www.rki.de/DE/Content/Infekt/Preparedness_Response/Rahmenkonzept_Epidemische_bedeutsame_Lagen.pdf?__blob=publicationFile (accessed January 12, 2021).

8. Miquel Porta (ed.), *A Dictionary of Epidemiology*, 6th edn. (Oxford: Oxford University Press, 2014).

9. World Health Organization, *Pandemic Influenza Risk Management*, https://www.who.int/influenza/preparedness/pandemic/influenza_risk_management_update2017/en (accessed January 12, 2021).

10. Act to Implement the International Health Regulations (2005) (IHR) of May 23, 2005, https://www.rki.de/DE/Content/Infekt/IGV/Gesetz_IGV_de-en.pdf?__blob=publicationFile (accessed January 12, 2021).

11. Hans Heesterbeek et al., "Modeling Infectious Disease Dynamics in the Complex Landscape of Global Health" in *Science* 347, (2015).

12. Alessandro Cassini, Burden of AMR Collaborative Group, "Attributable deaths and disability-adjusted life-years caused by infections with antibiotic-resistant bacteria in the EU and the European Economic Area in 2015: a population-level modelling analysis" in *The Lancet Infectious Diseases*, vol. 19, issue 1 (January 2019), pp. 56–66, doi: 10.1016/S1473-3099(18)30605-4.

13. Lothar H. Wieler, "What is the Real Threat of Pandemics?" in *Crossing Boundaries in Science* (2019); pp. 125–136, doi: 10.24395/01_0021.

14. Andrew T. Levin, William P. Hanage, Nana Owusu-Boaitey, Kensington B. Chochran, Seamus P. Walsh and Gideon Meyerowtiz-Katz, "Assessing the age specificity of infection fatality rates for COVID-19: systematic review, meta-analysis, and public policy implications" in *European Journal of Epidemiology* 35 (2020), pp. 1123–1138.

15. Lothar H. Wieler, "What is the Real Threat of Pandemics?"

16. https://www.rki.de/DE/Content/InfAZ/N/Neuartiges_Coronavirus/nCoV.html (accessed January 12, 2021).

17. https://www.rki.de/DE/Content/InfAZ/N/Neuartiges_Coronavirus/Intensivregister.html (accessed January 12, 2021).

18. Robert Koch Institute, *Rahmenkonzept.*

19. Robert Koch Institute, *Nationaler Pandemieplan Teil I.*

20. http://www.gesetze-im-internet.de/ifsg/index.html (accessed January 12, 2021).

21. Act to Implement the International Health Regulations (2005) (IHR) of May 23, 2005.

22. http://www.gesetze-im-internet.de/igv-dg (accessed January 12, 2021).

23. Joint External Evaluation, https://www.rki.de/DE/Content/Infekt/IGV/JEE.html (accessed January 12, 2021).

24. Robert Koch Institute, *Rahmenkonzept.*

25. https://extranet.who.int/goarn (accessed January 12, 2021).

26. https://www.rki.de/DE/Content/Institut/WHOCC/WHO_CC_GOARN_inhalt.html (accessed January 12, 2021).

27. Global Health Protection Programme, https://ghpp.de/de (accessed January 12, 2021).

28. IANPHI, https://www.ianphi.org (accessed January 12, 2021).

29. https://www.bundesgesundheitsministerium.de/service/begriffe-von-a-z/o/oeffentlicher-gesundheitsheitsdienst-pakt.html (accessed January 12, 2021).

30. Florian Dorn et al., "Das gemeinsame Interesse von Gesundheit und Wirtschaft: Eine Szenarienrechnung zur Eindämmung der Corona-Pandemie" in *ifo Schnelldienst Digital* (2020), 1, no. 06.

31. Juliet Bedford et al., "Living with the COVID-19 pandemic: act now with the tools we have, Comment" in *The Lancet* vol. 396, issue 10259 (2020), pp. 1314–1316, https://doi.org/10.1016/S0140-6736(20)32117-6 (accessed January 12, 2021).

CHAPTER 16

IS COVID-19 A GLOBAL TURNING POINT? SOME HISTORICAL PERSPECTIVES

JÖRN LEONHARD

Looking back from some point in the future, how will we have understood COVID-19?[1] What we are expressing here in the future perfect tense refers to the fundamental problem of what characterizes an empirical upheaval, or even an epoch-making threshold, and how historical turning points are created by the logic of hindsight, that is, by taking a retrospective view of medium- and long-term consequences. To do this, historians usually need longer experiential distances. Indeed, the term *ancien régime*, as applied to an era and as an analytical category referring to the period before the French Revolution, was not used in 1789, but was coined by skeptical writers in the 19th century. The French writer Alexis de Tocqueville and the Swiss historian Jacob Burckhardt were at least of the same opinion that their own present day in the 1840s, 1850s, and 1870s still belonged to the revolutionary era that may have begun with the events of 1789, but which stretched far beyond this year and other liminal dates such as 1799 or 1815. This structural change could not be encapsulated by chronological signposts that suggested a clear separation between before and after, a clarity that the revolution as a process with many non-simultaneous ramifications managed to escape.

So every prediction—not the domain of the historian, in any case—is conditional on more or less plausible speculation, formulated in a state of constant uncertainty. In the midst of a still unpredictable crisis, it is tempting to think of the impact of a global pandemic as a historical turning point, but the heuristic and hermeneutic ice is and will remain thin. Nevertheless, from a historical perspective there are at least a few preliminary observations that may help to give a sense of some elements of this confusing present. In so doing, we find no historical blueprints for crisis management in the present. Historical points of view are more likely to create a productive kind of alienation. The exploratory mode of knowledge in a crisis is not knowing better but seeing more. The following symptomatic observations by a historian are formulated with this perspective in mind.

1. THEMATIC ANALOGY: PANDEMIC AND WAR

Comparing pandemics with wars and revolutions, or at least with historical crises, suggests itself at a moment of acute threat to and a state of emergency in societies. And indeed, war metaphors dominated the initial political reactions to the COVID-19 crisis with suspicious frequency. Yet such comparisons smooth over the significant differences between a war and a pandemic, because unlike the virus, wars ultimately arise as the result of concrete political decision-making processes in human societies. The virus acquires the specific image of "enemy" only when attributed by people, an image that can extend to giving it an ethnic identity: for example in attributing supposed responsibility for the virus's spread and infection to certain countries.

2. CHRONOLOGICAL ANALOGY: COVID-19 AND
THE SPANISH FLU OF 1918–19

In current debates, reference is often made to the experience of Spanish flu at the end of World War I. But the differences between this historical event and the present are revealing.[2] The influenza pandemic at the end of World War I first struck Africa, Asia, the United States, and Latin America before finally reaching Europe at the end of the war. In many places the high number of victims revealed the extent to which people in the societies affected, both directly and indirectly by more than four years of war, were exhausted. Because the newspapers in neutral Spain were able to report the effects of the flu largely uncensored, the pandemic was named "Spanish flu." Effective remedies against the disease and, above all, the pneumonia that often accompanied it, were not available. Its leading pathogen, the H1N1 virus, was not identified until the 1990s.

Equally, in the case of 1918–19, the world-historical event of the Spanish flu only became apparent in retrospect. During the time of acute crisis in 1918–19, people did not know that the pandemic ultimately claimed more victims than the war in terms of military and civilian fatalities combined. This reflected a completely different global context by comparison with today, as people living a century ago were affected by many other upheavals on the military fronts and in their home societies, whether it was the end of the war, revolutions, or civil wars breaking out in many parts of Europe, the collapse of old empires such as the Tsarist regime, the Habsburg monarchy, and the Ottoman Empire, or the formation of new states. The postwar phase which had been anticipated again and again during the war, becoming a fervent dream of the future, now appeared both promising and threatening in its openness. Thus, the Spanish flu became the catastrophe that happened in the shadow of many parallel crises, while at the same time creating an invisible worldwide interdependency—globalized chains of infection and pathways of contamination—even before the armistice and peace conferences took place. For many people in wartime societies, the Spanish flu also evoked the soldier's fundamental wartime experiences—the constant proximity to death and the randomness of dying.

The COVID-19 pandemic that emerged at the end of 2019 did so not against the backdrop of a world war, which in 1918–19 had provided locations and epidemiological highways for spreading the disease in the form of training camps, field hospitals, and global troop transportation. Unlike today, there was hardly any shared expertise, no international health organization, no hourly updated and available data on the spread of the disease, or even a coordinated search for a vaccine. But as in 1918, the pandemic now also reveals the mechanisms of global currents and the extent of global interdependence—hence the focus on the global mobility of information and capital as well as of tourists and economic actors. In the first waves of infection, the pandemic could even be regarded as a disease of highly mobile globalization profiteers, for whom every travel ban must have seemed like a constraint to the basic freedoms they had enjoyed for so many years. Now we have seen, in another similarity with the Spanish flu, how severely the socially disadvantaged are being affected by the pandemic. As in 1919, COVID-19 reveals its own social hierarchy of victims.

3. POST-CORONA: "TRANSLATIO IMPERII"?

What does the COVID-19 pandemic mean for today's world order? Is it a trigger, a catalyst of processes whose origins precede the outbreak of the pandemic, or does the pandemic represent a new kind of cause for a qualitative change in today's geopolitical constellation, even a *translatio imperii*, i.e. the replacement of one world empire by another, or at least the prelude to a global rebalancing of power relations?

The creation of great empires, the consolidation and erosion of their power, as well as the *translatio imperii* as crises of replacement all have characterized historical processes for millennia. In history, global rises and falls and the associated changes in alliances are the norm. Out of the crisis of the Roman Empire, which resulted in the division between the Eastern and Western Empires, competing imperial ideas arose in Rome and Constantinople, supplemented since the 15th century and the Muslim conquest of the Eastern Empire by the translation of the Eastern Roman Empire's heritage to Moscow and Saint Petersburg, where the idea of a "Third Rome" developed. Sweden's displacement as an imperial power in northeastern Europe by Peter the Great's Russia enabled the rise of the Tsarist regime to the status of a major continental European power—this, too, was a *translatio imperii* by means of war. Ultimately, the upheavals of World Wars I and II accelerated the decline of the European system of five great powers, the Pentarchy of Great Britain, France, Russia, the Habsburg monarchy, and Prussia, whose transformation had, however, already begun at the end of the 19th century with the rise of the United States and Japan as non-European imperial actors. Between 1917 and 1923, while the continental European empires were disintegrating, the colonial empires of Great Britain and France expanded to their maximum extent as the territorial inheritance of Germany and the Ottoman Empire was divided up. In the late 20th century, the end of the Cold War in 1989–91 presented another imperial upheaval.

The idea of imperial hegemony has always been part of the thinking about the global political system, often linked to the empires' particular aspiration to peace, whether in the form of the Pax Romana in ancient Rome, the post-1648 interpretation of the Holy Roman Empire as a pacifying buffer zone in Europe, from which no war of aggression could arise, the Pax Britannica, Americana, and Sovietica in the 19th and 20th centuries, or today China's global promise of peace, welfare, and health, a facet of Beijing's self-image intended to demonstrate imperial strength.

After global political crises and upheavals, especially after the dissolution or fall of empires, we see the characteristic juxtaposition of a desire for a structuring system on the one hand and for simultaneous multipolarity on the other. This desire links the following periods, in spite of all their differences: after the end of the Napoleonic Wars and the Congress of Vienna in 1815; after the end of the Crimean War in 1856; after the establishment of the new Italian and German nation states in 1871; the periods after the world wars ended in 1918 and 1945; but also after the collapse of the Soviet Union and the end of the Cold War in 1989–91, and once again our present day. Such tentative movements and orientation processes are not in themselves new, but in the COVID-19 crisis they are much more evident than before. Some of these processes originated before the outbreak of the pandemic, with the result that their contours are now more defined and their developments are accelerated. In this situation, COVID-19 acts initially more as a catalyst rather than a major disruption, as an efficiency test that intensifies the global struggle for interpretive power in our media age of smartphones, artificial intelligence, and the rise of algorithms, but also as a test of legitimacy and loyalty.

We can identify three imperial narratives. First, the conflict between the United States and China as imperial powers wielding tools that are both classical and new. This includes the territory as a zone of influence and at the same time non-territorial currencies of power such as financial capital, knowledge, and the control of platform companies. These elements reinforce certain tendencies of the so-called "New Wars" that have been observed since the end of the Cold War, which are, above all, characterized by a de-contouring of conflicts. This occurs alongside the asymmetrical amalgamation of elements from state, civil, and religious wars, of warlordism, terror, and gang crime that prevail in the "New Wars."

In the case of China, alongside the focus on the East China Sea, the "New Silk Road" program, and Huawei, as a globally operating technology base, have emerged, while the authoritarian and repressive character of the regime is clear in Hong Kong and in China's way of dealing with ethnic and religious minorities. For the Chinese elite, this self-image is not at all about the "rise" of their own country, which primarily dominates in European and transatlantic perceptions, but rather about a return to China's imperial origins in the premodern era, before the "Great Divergence" that resulted in the socio-economic dominance of Western societies after the 18th century and the European colonial powers' humiliation of China in the 19th and early 20th centuries.

Second, today's project of European integration and the European Union can be described as a "benevolent empire" that does not wage offensive wars and which has succeeded in keeping the peace in continental Europe, historically an area of intense conflict, on a permanent basis. After 1945, Europe's integration enabled lasting peace and stability on the continent not least through the incorporation of the Federal Republic of Germany, through the integration of Greece, Spain, and Portugal after periods of authoritarianism and dictatorship in the 1970s, and finally through the gradual inclusion of the Central, Eastern, and Southeastern European states after 1989–90. However, these past successes were subsequently thrown into crisis with the break-up of Yugoslavia and the escalation of ethnic violence. Today we can see further symptoms of crisis, be it through systemic competition with external authoritarian and populist regimes or through internal crises caused by Great Britain's exit from the Union, as well as by the controversies over the implementation of democratic and constitutional norms in Eastern European Member States. In Eastern Ukraine, Syria, and North Africa, the limits of the European Union's effectiveness as an agent for peace are evident.

Third and finally, today we can discern trends towards the establishment of new imperial orders after the end of the Cold War and under the aegis of a new multipolarity, whether in Turkey's neo-Ottoman policies, which are accentuated in historical, political, and religious terms in the repurposing of the Hagia Sophia, or in Russia's alignment with its imperial past, as can be seen clearly in the celebration of May 8, 1945, and the deliberate promise to protect Russian Orthodoxy. In these contexts, imperiality not only means the politics of memory, but also acquires a very concrete dimension in territorial claims and their associated interventions, such as in Crimea, Eastern Ukraine, Syria, and Libya.

Will we ultimately undergo a new *translatio imperii*, the transition from the "Imperium Americanum" to a Chinese imperial century? Whatever happens, the COVID-19 crisis has considerably exacerbated the conflict between these two imperial powers, creating a new great power rivalry. If an empire is defined by size, duration, and a normative mission, then the United States' self-image as the new Jerusalem with the aim of democratizing the world is under considerable internal and external pressure, as became apparent in the crisis-ridden escalation of Donald Trump's presidency and China's simultaneous re-focus on its own imperial past, as well as on its promise of strength, welfare, and health, a conscious reference to China's narrative proclaiming the weakness of Western democracies.

4. GLOBALIZATION, DEGLOBALIZATION, "GLOCALITY"

Already after the turning point of World War I, an interplay between globalization and deglobalization emerged, which will likely also characterize the post-COVID-19 era as a geopolitical rebalancing of powers. The 1920s and 1930s became an example of the coexistence of global cooperation and international interdependence on the one hand, with isolation and separation on the other. While the United States was able to achieve unprecedented global impact in financial and economic policy through the outcome of the world war—from the Dawes and Young Plans through the Hoover Moratorium to the mitigation of German reparations payments as a core problem of the postwar period—after the non-ratification of the Versailles Treaty and the League of Nations and the failure of the internationalism personified by American President Woodrow Wilson, the US government appealed to an early version of "America First." After 1919, this movement was associated domestically with racial exclusion, which was reflected in severe racial unrest causing hundreds of deaths and a new, anti-Bolshevik bogeyman in the "Red Summer" of 1919, as well as in intensified immigration policies externally.

Historically, after profound experiences of crisis, structural globalization, typified by the revolution in communications technology such as the telegraph in the 19th century and the internet in the 20th, and sectoral anti-globalization or deglobalization, such as the rejection of the rule of law and democracy, often went hand in hand. Both trends complemented and mutually reinforced each other, for example by invoking universal tendencies to enhance individual agency and specific responses respectively, that is in the paradox of a "glocal" constellation. A particularly impressive example of this was the history of the new idea of national self-determination formulated after 1917 by US President Woodrow Wilson and the Russian Bolsheviks in contrast to the balance of powers and the tradition of secret diplomacy: self-determination became a global word for empowerment, provoking local expectations, however, in each case and reflecting the individual margins for maneuver.

This "glocal" constellation also applied to the period after the end of the Cold War. On the one hand, supranational integration accelerated the erosion of nation states' traditional concept of sovereignty, especially in Europe. The established nation state of the 19th century lost its importance within the European Union as a result of movements coming from two directions:

transfers of sovereignty in the context of progressive European integration and, at the same time, new kinds of regionalism, which, as in Scotland or Catalonia, sometimes escalated into independence movements.

On the other hand, the nation state continues to act as an important, and in many places crucial, political, legal, and emotional benchmark in times of crisis, whether in guaranteeing savings as in the financial crisis after 2008, in calling for borders to be closed during the refugee crisis in 2015, or in the expectation of government crisis management and preparations during the current COVID-19 pandemic. It is at least probable that the historical tension between different globalization processes and deglobalization will remain with us.

5. NEW NATIONALISMS AS A RESULT OF RETERRITORIALIZATION

If we examine reactions after the outbreak of the pandemic, we are reminded of the words of the Swiss writer Max Frisch, when he wrote that nature recognizes no catastrophes—only humans can recognize catastrophes, provided they survive them.[3] This affects the interpretive level, whether as analysis, scenario, prophecy, plan, or forecast. The infection has created and continues to create profound and persistent uncertainty, because the traditional instruments of crisis management are at least called into question. At the time of immediate threat, appeals to the initially nationally defined health and welfare state dominated. This is where the aforementioned dichotomy between global challenges and specific answers is particularly evident.

Beyond objectifiable facts and scientifically verified statements, the factors giving guidance for action have been subjective perceptions, including their manipulations and distortions. Therefore, the fact that the virus recognizes neither national classification nor national borders says nothing about the reaction of people whose actions are prefigured more robustly by traditional patterns of interpretation. The nation state's promise of protection as a health and hygiene state is part of this, even in the shrill version of conspiracy theories or in the attribution of blame to certain ethnically defined groups as supposed "carriers"—a reaction that sometimes echoes how supposed "enemy aliens" were treated during the world wars.

If the pattern of reactions to crises of the past, such as the financial crisis after 2008 and especially the refugee crisis of 2015, revealed a kind of nationalism with ethnic connotations, the COVID-19 crisis has instead

shown a tendency towards situational renationaliza-
tion as setting out one's territory—a tendency towards
reterritorialization. Borders that were suddenly closed
and states' aspirations to cut off familiar ties through
control and discipline, based equally on the definition
of a critical state of emergency, and to define "protection," "contagion," "risk" and access to vaccinations
in territorial terms, seemed like a kind of atavism in
light of the permeability of many borders in Europe
up until the pandemic's outbreak. Even if a complete
abandonment of globalization is hardly conceivable,
these experiences will give rise to different economic
processes. The individual state will not rely on efficient
global supply chains alone, but also on resilient logis-
tics and the reduction of sectoral dependency through
more strategic stockpiling. Faced with becoming the
vulnerable link in a global supply chain, the state as a
warehouse will gain importance.

In this regard, COVID-19 reinforces a kind of
reterritorialized nationalism in which, as outlined
above, it is no coincidence that older imperial tradi-
tions are evoked—it is just as noticeable in Chinese
state propaganda about the "New Silk Road" and in
China's dealings with Hong Kong and Taiwan as it is in
Russia's approach to the Crimea, to Eastern Ukraine,
and to Syria, as well as in Turkey, with its mixture of

politicized Islam and an emphatically anti-Western promise of strength.

6. PARADOXICAL CONSTELLATIONS AS THE IMAGE OF A FLUID PRESENT

Living with COVID-19, today's world is increasingly proving to be an agglomeration of paradoxical constellations, which is not uncommon in the case of historical crises.[4] They provide a particular view of certain developments, achievements, and legacies that have occurred over the last few years and decades. There is some evidence that these initial paradoxes will also remain with us into the near future. This includes, first of all, the juxtaposition of knowledge and ignorance about the pandemic, of information about routes of infection, disease progression, and treatment methods being shared globally while in a state of ignorance about realistic types of medication, the long-term consequences of illness, phases of immunity, and the economic and political consequences of the pandemic.

In addition, in the context of government reactions, border closures, lockdowns, and emergency regimes, we get the feeling that our power to act is restricted and our personal freedoms severely limited, which at the same time results in a powerful awareness of the value of these very freedoms as well as in a highly self-confident reclamation of public space, for example. While the individual's power to act was initially restricted, many citizens have, beyond conspiracy narratives and extremisms, developed a critical awareness of state institutions and elites who are banking on a simple return to the old system. In other words, in a time of crisis, citizens hold their state to a measure of efficiency that has been radicalized by insecurity, a criterion that increases their sensitivity to the restriction of individual rights.

Ultimately, the above-mentioned juxtaposition of globalization and deglobalization is also part of the paradox of the present: in addition to globalism as an epidemiological prerequisite for the spread of viruses and the global dimension of the challenge, there are specific responses, reinforced in Germany by its federal and municipal constitution and its new emphasis on the principle of subsidiarity. Primarily, the juxtaposition of global and local responses to the COVID-19 pandemic means that comparisons are being permanently drawn, thus creating a latent form of competition between successful and unsuccessful virus containment in different municipalities, districts, federal states, European states, and countries throughout the world.

7. A TEST OF LEGITIMACY WHEN DRAWING GLOBAL COMPARISONS

Against this backdrop, we cannot make a simple causal connection between the experience of a crisis and trends towards authoritarianism, a connection that was often made in the early phase of the crisis, frequently in analogy with the period after World War I. But the COVID-19 crisis is not happening under conditions created by politics; it is not an easy fit for dictatorships. Rather, it seems that incremental disenchantment with authoritarian regimes and neo-imperial claims intensifies if the latter do not meet societies' expectations of efficiency and undermine the problem-solving skills that are required. This is exactly where globalism, operating on the basis of available and shareable knowledge, data, and news, intensifies the comparisons.

We could cite other paradoxes: for example, the simultaneities of absence and presence, growth and contraction, experiences that are shared while at the same time societies are domestically polarized, rational focus alongside a high degree of emotion.

So where have we arrived? Identifying a turning point involves pinning down the pluperfect tense. However, the COVID-19 pandemic does not yet have a definable *ancien régime*. Nevertheless, the multitude of paradoxes we have outlined increases the likelihood of a world in upheaval, between transition and transformation, not created through a hiatus like a revolution in a single moment, but incrementally through the gradual unfolding and ever longer duration of the crisis. One thing is that we perceive a lot of familiar things in what is supposedly new: we can now identify the crises of the European Union or the Sino-American imperial tension more precisely through the problem of the pandemic. But at the same time, we can today no longer be as certain as we were a year ago that something completely new isn't emerging from beneath the surface of the supposedly familiar, the apparently repetitive, the prefigured present, breaking through the hermeneutical framework of the narrative of continuity.

When in January 2020 journalists at *Der Spiegel* magazine commissioned a short text to mark the beginning of the new decade, the German playwright and essayist Botho Strauß wrote:

Among the many visions of the future predicted for
the 20th century almost none of the great global trans-
formations appears: no contraceptive pills, no aging
of the West European population, no German reuni-
fication, no digital revolution. The most important
things came along unexpectedly. The future, what
is to come, is only rarely the fulfillment of what has
long been looming or longed for. The historiography
of induction is now a questionable methodology. We
should just try to write the history of emergences and
inconsistencies. We should distinguish the disruptive
from the evolving, discover that event in history that
happens without advance notice or preparation. The
emergentist—who will have absolutely nothing more
to do with continuity—will no longer describe the
future as such [...][5]

Notes

1. Cf. Jörn Leonhard, "Post-Corona: Über historische
   Zäsurbildung unter den Bedingungen der Unsicherheit"
   in Bernd Kortmann and Günther G. Schulze (eds.), *Jenseits
   von Corona. Unsere Welt nach der Pandemie – Perspektiven aus
   der Wissenschaft* (Bielefeld: Transcript Verlag, 2020), pp.
   197–203.

2. Jörn Leonhard, *Der überforderte Frieden. Versailles und die
   Welt 1918–1923*, 2nd. edn. (Munich: C.H. Beck, 2019), pp.
   11–15.

3. Max Frisch, *Man in the Holocene*, trans. Geoffrey Skelton
   (Dallas, TX: Dalkey Archive Press, 2009), p. 79.

4. Lothar Gorris and Ivan Krastev, "Wir sehen, was wir vorher nicht sehen konnten," *Spiegel-Gespräch* in *Der Spiegel* 27, June 27, 2020, p. 120.

5. Botho Strauß, "Das Wichtigste kam unvorhergesehen" in *Der Spiegel* 1, December 28, 2019, p. 114.

CONTRIBUTORS

Dr. Maha Hosain Aziz is a professor, author and cartoonist in global risk and prediction at NYU's MA International Relations Program and a risk expert in the World Economic Forum's Global Future Council. She has written two books: award-winning best-seller *Future World Order: A Global Legitimacy Crisis in the 2020s* (2020) (15 percent of profits go to her brother's memorial fund for Syrian refugee youth in Jordan's Za'atari camp) and its sequel, *A Global Spring: Navigating a Post-Pandemic World* (2021) (50 percent of profits to the WHO's COVID-19 Solidarity Response Fund). She also drew the award-winning political comic book *The Global Kid* (2016) (all profits to education charities), which is being launched as a VR/AR political comic book for tweens in spring 2021.

CONTRIBUTORS

Univ. Prof. em. Dr. sc. tc. hc. Bazon Brock, thinker at large and artist without portfolio, is Emeritus Professor of Aesthetics and Cultural Education at the Bergische Universität in Wuppertal, Germany. Other professorships include at Hamburg University of Fine Arts (1965–76) and the University of Applied Arts, Vienna (1977–80). In 1992 he was awarded an honorary doctorate at ETH (Swiss Federal Institute for Technology, Zürich) and in 2012 at the Hochschule für Gestaltung, Karlsruhe. Since 2014 he has been Honorary Professor for Prophecy at HBKsaar (Saar College of Fine Arts), Saarbrücken. In 2016 he was awarded the Von der Heydt Prize by the City of Wuppertal and in 2017 the Austrian Cross of Honour for Science and Art. He has developed the method of "Action Teaching," in which the seminar hall becomes a place of enactment, for oneself and others. Between 1968 and 1992, he led the documenta schools for visitors, which he founded in Kassel. From 2010 to 2013 he ran courses for "professional citizens" at the Karlsruhe University of Arts and Design. He has organized around 3,000 events and "action plays," e.g. *Lustmarsch durchs Theoriegelände* (2006, in eleven museums). He is a member of the Institut für theoretische Kunst, Universalpoesie und Prognostik, and Founder of the Amt für Arbeit an unlösbaren

Problemen und Maßnahmen der hohen Hand, Berlin (www.denkerei-berlin.de).

Prof. Dr. Garrett Wallace Brown is Chair of Global Health Policy and Co-Director of the Global Health Research Theme at the University of Leeds. He has published widely on global health governance and policy, health financing, health systems strengthening and global health security, with a particular research interest in African health and development policy. He has acted as a policy expert for the media at the G7 and G20 Leaders Summits and has acted as a scientific advisor for a number of governmental and non-governmental health organizations. Professor Brown also conducts research in political theory and legal philosophy, which includes work on cosmopolitanism, global constitutionalism, and the political philosophy of Immanuel Kant. His recent non-medical publications include *The State and Cosmopolitan Responsibilities* (2019) and *Kant's Cosmopolitics* (2019). His work on COVID-19 has been published in the *British Medical Journal* (2020).

Prof. Dr. Eugénia da Conceição-Heldt has held the chair of European and Global Governance at the Bavarian School of Public Policy / TUM School of Governance since July 2016. Her research interests include the delegation of power to international organizations, European integration, global economic governance, two-level games, negotiation analysis, and accountability in global governance.

She received her Ph.D. in Political Science from the Freie Universität Berlin and completed her post-doctoral qualification at the Humboldt-Universität zu Berlin. From March 2012 through June 2016 she held the chair of International Politics at TU Dresden. Previous appointments include a guest professorship at the FU Berlin, an assistant professorship at HU Berlin, and fellowships at the Center for European Studies at Harvard University, at the European University Institute in Florence (EUI), and at the Social Science Research Center Berlin (WZB). She is the author of over 20 peer-reviewed journal articles and four monographs, several books and has edited special issues for peer-reviewed journals and book chapters. Her research has been published in journals such as *Journal of Common Market Studies, Journal of European Public Policy, Negotiation Journal, International Negotiations, International Politics, Journal of Comparative Policy Analysis, Global Society* and *Politische Vierteljahresschrift.*

Prof. Dr. Dr. Udo Di Fabio began his professional career in Dinslaken, North Rhine-Westphalia in 1970 as a middle-grade municipal administrator. During this time, he went back to school to complete his high school graduation, subsequently studying jurisprudence at Ruhr-Universität Bochum and the social sciences at Duisburg University (today the University of Duisburg-Essen). After passing state examinations in law in 1982 and 1985, Prof. Dr. Dr. Udo Di Fabio worked initially as a Judge at the Duisburg Court of Social Welfare, before, in 1986, becoming a Research Assistant at the Institute of Public Law at the Rhenisch University of Bonn. He completed his doctoral thesis there one year later, and in 1990 he wrote a doctoral thesis in the social sciences. In 1993, after completing his postdoctoral research, he was appointed Professor of Public Law at the University of Münster, and a few months later he accepted an appointment at the University of Trier. Between 1997 and 2003 Prof. Dr. Dr. Udo Di Fabio taught at Ludwig-Maximilian University Munich. Since 2003 he has been Professor of Public Law at the Rhenisch Friedrich Wilhelm University of Bonn. On December 16, 1999 Prof. Dr. Dr. Udo Di Fabio was appointed Justice of the Second Senate in Germany's Federal Constitutional Court. His department covered in particular European law, international law, and parliamentary law. He continues to teach and research in Bonn and since 2016 he is founding director of the *Forschungskolleg normative Gesellschaftsgrundlagen* (https://www.forschungskolleg.eu).

Dr. Corinne Michaela Flick studied both law and literature, taking American studies as her subsidiary, at Ludwig Maximilian University, Munich. She gained her Dr. Phil. in 1989. She has worked as in-house lawyer for Bertelsmann Buch AG and Amazon.com. In 1998 she became General Partner in Vivil GmbH und Co. KG, Offenburg. She is Founder and Chair of the Convoco Foundation. As Editor of Convoco! Editions she has published among others: *The Standing of Europe in the New Imperial World Order* (Convoco! Editions, 2020), *The Multiple Futures of Capitalism* (Convoco! Editions, 2019), *The Common Good in the 21st Century* (Convoco! Editions, 2018), *Authority in Transformation* (Convoco! Editions, 2017), *Power and its Paradoxes* (Convoco! Editions, 2016), *To Do or Not To Do—Inaction as a Form of Action* (Convoco! Editions, 2015), *Dealing with Downturns: Strategies in Uncertain Times* (Convoco! Editions, 2014), and *Collective Lawbreaking—A Threat to Liberty* (Convoco! Editions, 2013). In 2019 Corinne

Flick became the Chair of the Board of Ambassadors at the ESMT Berlin.

Prof. Dr. Dr. h.c. Clemens Fuest gained his doctorate at the University of Cologne in 1994 and his postdoctoral qualification at Ludwig-Maximilian University Munich in 2001, when he was appointed Professor of Political Economy at the University of Cologne, until 2008, and Visiting Professor at Bocconi University in Milan. From 2008 to 2013 he was Professor of Business Taxation and Research Director of the University of Oxford Centre for Business Taxation. Between 2013 and March 2016 he was President and Director of Science and Research of the Centre for European Economic Research (ZEW) and Professor of Economics at the University of Mannheim. Since April 2016 he has been President of the Ifo Institute for Economic Research in Munich.

He is among other posts a member of the Academic Advisory Board of the German Federal Ministry of Finance, the European Academy of Sciences and Arts as well as the Academic Advisory Board of Ernst & Young GmbH. Furthermore, he is a member of the Minimum Wage Committee of the Federal Republic of Germany. Until 2017 he belonged to the "High Level Group on Own Resources" (Monti-Commission) of the European Union. In 2013 he received the Gustav Stolper Award of the Verein für Socialpolitik (Social Policies Society – VfS), in 2019 the Hanns Martin Schleyer Award. He is a member of numerous learned academies in Germany and internationally, and has been President of the International Institute for Public Finance since 2019. Clemens Fuest has published a number of books and articles in national and international journals. He also regularly contributes to public debates on economic and fiscal policy with articles in renowned newspapers as the *Handelsblatt, Frankfurter Allgemeine Zeitung, Süddeutsche Zeitung, Wirtschaftswoche* and *The Wall Street Journal.*

Prof. Dr. Stefan Korioth gained his doctorate in law in 1990 and completed his postdoctoral qualification in public and constitutional law. From 1996 to 2000 he was Professor of Public Law, Constitutional History, and Theory of Government at the University of Greifswald. In 2000 he accepted the Chair of Public and Ecclesiastical Law at Ludwig Maximilian University Munich. His publications include *Integration und Bundesstaat* (1990), *Der Finanzausgleich zwischen Bund und Ländern* (1997), *Grundzüge des Staatskirchenrechts* (with B. Jean d'Heur, 2000), *Das*

Bundesverfassungsgericht (with Klaus Schlaich, 11th edition, 2018), and *Staatsrecht I* (5th edition, 2020).

Prof. Dr. Jörn Leonhard is Chair of Western European History at the Albert Ludwig University of Freiburg, and an author. Having studied history, political science, and German philology in Heidelberg and Oxford, he received his Ph.D. in 1998 and completed his postdoctoral qualification at Heidelberg University in 2004. From 1998 to 2003 he was a Fellow and Tutor at Oxford University; Visiting Research Fellow at the Alexander von Humboldt Foundation in the German–American Center for Visiting Scholars in Washington, D.C. in 2001; Fellow of the Royal Historical Society London since 2002; and Senior Fellow at the Institute for Contemporary History of the Historisches Kolleg in Munich from 2016 to 2017. From 2007 to 2012 he was Director of the School of History at the Freiburg Institute for Advanced Studies (FRIAS) and in 2012/13 Visiting Professor at Harvard University. His research and publications have received multiple awards. His most recent English publication is *Pandora's Box: A History of the First World War* (2018). Jörn Leonhard has been full member of the Heidelberg Academy of Sciences and Humanities since 2015 and Honorary Fellow of Wadham College, Oxford University, since 2019.

Prof. Dr. h.c. Rudolf Mellinghoff studied at the University of Münster and served his postgraduate legal internship in Baden-Württemberg. Between 1984 and 1987 he was a Research Assistant at the University of Heidelberg, becoming a Judge in the Finance Court of Düsseldorf in 1987. From 1987 to 1991 he was a Research Fellow at the Federal Constitutional Court. He was appointed Judge at the Finance Court of Düsseldorf in 1989. Rudolf Mellinghoff was Head of Department at the Ministry of Justice of Mecklenburg-Vorpommern between July 1991 and June 1992, and was appointed Presiding Judge of the Finance Court in 1996. In a second full-time position, he served as Judge of the Higher Administrative Court of Mecklenburg-Vorpommern between 1992 and 1996. From 1995 to 1996 he was also a member of the Constitutional Court of Mecklenburg-Vorpommern, and from 1997 to 2001 served as Judge at the German Federal Court of Auditors. From January 2001 to October 2011 Rudolf Mellinghoff served as Justice in the Second Senate of the Federal Constitutional Court. He then served as the President of the Federal Court of Auditors until July 2020. In 2006 Rudolf Mellinghoff was awarded an

Honorary Doctorate from the University of Greifswald, and in 2007 from the Eberhard Karls University in Tübingen. In 2011 he was awarded the Grand Merit Cross with Star and Sash of the Order of Merit of the Federal Republic of Germany. From 2009 to 2011 he was President of the German Section of the International Commission of Jurists, becoming Vice-President in 2012. He was Chair of the Deutsche Steuerjuristische Gesellschaft 2011 to 2017 and Vice Chair in 2018. Currently, Rudolf Mellinghoff is Chair of the Advisory Council of the Berliner Steuergespräche e.V., Chair of the Judicial Integrity Group, member of the Permanent Scientific Committee of the International Fiscal Association (FIA), and member of the European Academy of Sciences and Arts (Academia Scientiarum et Artium Europaea).

Prof. Dr. Timo Meynhardt holds the Dr. Arend Oetker Chair of Business Psychology and Leadership at the HHL Leipzig Graduate School of Management. He is Managing Director of the Center for Leadership and Values in Society at the University of St. Gallen, where he obtained his doctorate and postdoctoral qualification in business administration. For several years, he was Practice Expert at McKinsey & Company. Timo Meynhardt's work focuses on public value management and leadership, combining psychology and business management in his research and teaching. He is co-developer of the Leipzig leadership model and co-publisher of the *Public Value Atlas* for Switzerland and Germany, which aims at making transparent the social benefits of companies and organizations (www. gemeinwohlatlas.de; www. gemeinwohl.ch). His Public Value Scorecard provides a management tool to measure and analyze the creation of public value. He is also Co-founder and Jury Member of the Public Value Awards for Startups.

Dr. Stefan Oschmann is Chairman of the Executive Board and CEO of Merck. Before taking office at the end of April 2016, he served as Vice-Chairman and Deputy CEO, with responsibility for Group Strategy, among other things. Stefan Oschmann joined Merck in 2011 as a member of the Executive Board and was responsible for the healthcare business sector until the end of 2014. He drove the transformation of the biopharma business by optimizing its cost structures and improving the efficiency of its research and development model, which included a clear portfolio prioritization. Before joining Merck, Stefan Oschmann worked for the US pharma company MSD, where he served in a range of senior executive positions. He started his career at an agency of the United Nations, and worked for the German Chemical Industry Association (VCI). Stefan Oschmann holds a doctorate in veterinary medicine from Ludwig Maximilian University in Munich.

Prof. em. Dr. Christoph G. Paulus studied law at Munich, taking his doctorate in law in 1980. His post-doctoral qualification, gained in 1991, was in civil law, civil procedure, and Roman law, for which he was awarded the Medal of the University of Paris II. Between 1989 and 1990 he was a recipient of a Feodor Lynen Stipend from the Humboldt Foundation in Berkeley, from which he had earlier gained his LL.M. From 1992 to 1994 he was Associate Professor at Augsburg, and from the summer semester 1994 he was at the Law Faculty of Humboldt University in Berlin, becoming Dean of the Faculty 2008–10. He is Consultant to the International Monetary Fund and the World Bank. Among other roles, he is a member of the International Insolvency Institute of the American College of Bankruptcy and the International Association for Procedural Law. From 2006 to 2010 he was advisor on insolvency law to the German delegation to UNCITRAL. He is on the editorial board of the *Zeitschrift für Wirtschaftsrecht* (ZIP), the *Northern*

Annual Review of International Insolvency, and the *International Insolvency Law Review*.

Gisbert Rühl has been CEO of the corporation Klöckner & Co since 2005 after having held several leading positions in industry and in consulting. He was initially Financial Manager, and since 2009 he has been Chairman of the Executive Board. Currently, Gisbert Rühl is advancing the digital transformation of Klöckner & Co as well as the development of an independent industry platform, XOM Materials, in which the company plays a pioneering role in the industry. He is furthermore involved in various organizations, for example, being a board member of the Society of Friends of Bayreuth, and takes a leading role in multiple initiatives of the World Economic Forum.

Prof. Dr. Dr. h.c. Wolfgang Schön studied law and economics at the University of Bonn. He was Professor at the University of Bielefeld from 1992 to 1996, and from 1996 to 2002 at the University of Bonn. Since 2002 he has been Director and Scientific Member of the Max Planck Institute for Tax Law and Public Finance in Munich. He is Honorary Professor at Ludwig Maximilian University Munich; member of the Global Law Faculty, New York University; and

International Research Fellow, University of Oxford Centre of Business Taxation. From 2008 to 2014 Prof. Schön was Vice-President of the Max Planck Society. Since 2014 he has been Vice-President of the German Research Foundation (DFG). He has published numerous works on German and European company law, competition law, and tax law.

Prof. Dr. Sven Simon is Chair of International Law, European Law, and Public Law at the Philipps University Marburg and since 2019 a Member of the European Parliament. Born in 1978, he studied law at the Justus Liebig University Gießen and at the University of Warwick, UK. He completed the first state legal examination in 2005 and received his doctorate in 2009. Following his practical legal training in Frankfurt, Berlin, Tel Aviv, and New York, he finished his second state legal examination in 2010. Sven Simon then returned to the Justus Liebig University Gießen to work as Academic Advisor for five years. In 2015 he was awarded his postdoctoral qualification for work on constitutional law analyzing the limits of the German Federal Court in the European integration process. After visiting professorships at the Free University Berlin and the University of Wisconsin, USA, he went on to an appointment at the Philipps University

Marburg in 2016. Sven Simon is Deputy Chair of the United Nations Association of Germany.

Prof. Dr. Lothar H. Wieler is President of the Robert Koch Institute in Berlin. From 1998 to 2015 he was University Professor for Microbiology and Animal Disease Studies at the Freie Universität Berlin. His research focuses on the "One Health" approach with an emphasis on zoonoses (diseases that are transmitted between animals and humans). In his research, he is interested in the molecular mechanisms that enable bacterial zoonotic pathogens to infect different hosts. His focus is on antibiotic-resistant and multi-resistant bacteria. Lothar Wieler is the author of over 250 scientific publications and has received several scientific prizes. He is co-founder of the German Research Platform for Zoonoses, and Deputy Spokesman of the InfectControl 2020 project consortium, which researches trans-sectoral approaches to infection prophylaxis and intervention in the "One Health" approach. He is also, among other posts, a member of the STAG-IH (Strategic and Technical Advisory Group for Infectious Hazards) of the World Health Organization, the EACHR (WHO Europe Advisory Committee on Health Research), and member of the advisory board of Technology, Methods, and

Infrastructure for Networked Medical Research
(TMF). He is the spokesman for the InfectControl
2020 consortia IRMRESS (innovative reduction of
multi-resistant infectious agents [MRE] and establishment of a next-generation sequencing-based molecular surveillance) and Neobiom (factors influencing
the development of micro-, resistor- and mycobiome
in premature infants). Before that, Wieler was the
spokesman for the BMBF joint project FBI-Zoo
(Foodborne Zoonotic Infections in Humans) and the
International DFG Research Training Group 1673
(Functional Molecular Infection Epidemiology).
Since 2010 Wieler has been an elected member of the
German National Academy of Sciences Leopoldina,
where he has served as a Senator since 2016.

THE STANDING OF EUROPE IN THE NEW IMPERIAL WORLD ORDER
2020

ISBN: 978-1-9163673-0-2

With contributions by: Fredrik Erixon, Gabriel Felbermayr, Birke Häcker, Matthias Karl, Parag Khanna, Kai A. Konrad, Stefan Korioth, Jörn Leonhard, Timo Meynhardt, Hans Ulrich Obrist with Edi Rama, Stefan Oschmann, Christoph G. Paulus, Rupprecht Podszun, Jörg Rocholl, Sven Simon, Yael Tamir, Roberto Viola, Claudia Wiesner

THE MULTIPLE FUTURES OF CAPITALISM
2019

ISBN: 978-0-9931953-8-9

With contributions by: Lucio Baccaro, Jens Beckert, Bazon Brock, Corinne M. Flick, Sean Hagan, Kai A. Konrad, Stefan Korioth, Justin Yifu Lin, Rudolf Mellinghoff, Timo Meynhardt, Hans Ulrich Obrist with Adam Curtis, Stefan Oschmann, Christoph G. Paulus, Herbert A. Reitsamer, Albrecht Ritschl, Jörg Rocholl, Gisbert Rühl, Monika Schnitzer, Wolfgang Schön

THE COMMON GOOD IN THE 21st CENTURY
2018

ISBN: 978-0-9931953-6-5

With contributions by: Roland Berger, Bazon Brock, Udo Di Fabio, Carl Benedikt Frey, Clemens Fuest, Kai A. Konrad, Stefan Korioth, Rudolf Mellinghoff, Timo Meynhardt, Hans Ulrich Obrist with Hito Steyerl and Matteo Pasquinelli, Stefan Oschmann, Christoph G. Paulus, Jörg Rocholl, Wolfgang Schön, Jens Spahn

AUTHORITY IN TRANSFORMATION
2017

ISBN: 978-0-9931953-4-1

With contributions by: Claudia Buch, Clemens Fuest, Thomas Hoeren, Peter M. Huber, Kai A. Konrad, Stefan Korioth, Peter Maurer, Hans Ulrich Obrist and Richard Wentworth, Stefan Oschmann, Christoph G. Paulus, Roger Scruton, Wolfgang Schön

POWER AND ITS PARADOXES
2016

ISBN: 978-0-9931953-2-7

With contributions by: Clemens Fuest, Thomas Hoeren, Wolfgang Ischinger, Stefan Korioth, Hans Ulrich Obrist and Simon Denny, Christoph G. Paulus, Albrecht Ritschl, Jörg Rocholl, Roger Scruton, Brendan Simms

TO DO OR NOT TO DO—INACTION AS A FORM OF ACTION
2015

ISBN: 978-0-9931953-0-3

With contributions by: Bazon Brock, Gert-Rudolf Flick, Peter M. Huber, Kai A. Konrad, Stefan Korioth, Friedhelm Mennekes, Hans Ulrich Obrist and Marina Abramović, Christoph G. Paulus, Jörg Rocholl, Wolfgang Schön, Roger Scruton, Pirmin Stekeler-Weithofer

DEALING WITH DOWNTURNS: STRATEGIES IN UNCERTAIN TIMES

2014

ISBN: 978-0-9572958-8-9

With contributions by: Jens Beckert, Bazon Brock, Saul David, Gerd Gigerenzer, Paul Kirchhof, Kai A. Konrad, Stefan Korioth, Christoph G. Paulus, Jörg Rocholl, Burkhard Schwenker

COLLECTIVE LAW-BREAKING—A THREAT TO LIBERTY

2013

ISBN: 978-0-9572958-5-8

With contributions by: Shaukat Aziz, Roland Berger, Christoph G. Paulus, Ingolf Pernice, Wolfgang Schön, Hannes Siegrist, Jürgen Stark, Pirmin Stekeler-Weithofer

WHO OWNS THE WORLD'S KNOWLEDGE?
2012

ISBN: 978-0-9572958-0-3

With contributions by: Eckhard Cordes, Urs Gasser, Thomas Hoeren, Viktor Mayer-Schönberger, Christoph G. Paulus, Jürgen Renn, Burkhard Schwenker, Hannes Siegrist

CAN'T PAY, WON'T PAY? SOVEREIGN DEBT AND THE CHALLENGE OF GROWTH IN EUROPE
2011

ISBN: 978-0-9572958-3-4

With contributions by: Roland Berger, Howard Davies, Otmar Issing, Paul Kirchhof, Kai A. Konrad, Stefan Korioth, Christoph G. Paulus, Burkhard Schwenker